FORAGE & EAT WITH THE SEASONS

A Recipe and Foraging Guide
to Wild Ingredients
and Sustainable Cooking

RAEANNA LAYFIELD

FORAGE & EAT WITH THE SEASONS
A Recipe and Foraging Guide to Wild Ingredients and Sustainable Cooking

Copyright © 2024 Raeanna Layfield

Photographs by Corrie Jelier, Matt Law, Adele Hinkley, Victoria Jackson, Raeanna Layfield, Adam Tavender & Robin from West Coast Mycology, Patrik Bogdan

All rights reserved. No part of this publication may be reproduced, distributed, or transmitted in any form or by any means, including photocopying, recording, or other electronic or mechanical means without proper written permission of the author or publisher, except in the case of brief quotations embodied in critical reviews and certain other noncommercial uses permitted by copyright law.

Printed in Canada
Paperback ISBN: 978-1-7380284-2-9
Hardback ISBN: 978-1-7380284-1-2

Published By

TPP
THE PUBLISHING PAD

The Publishing Pad
www.thepublishingpad.com

Coho Salmon

Disclaimers

- **Do not use this book as a species identification guide.** Some plants and fungi are harmful, even deadly, if touched or ingested. Distinguishing between dangerous species and safe ones requires training, and this book is not intended as a training manual for species identification. Readers are responsible for finding and using appropriate resources for safe foraging, including but not limited to region-specific guidebooks and in-person, expert-led tours of foraging sites. The author is not a botanist or horticulturalist.
- **Consult a physician before applying or ingesting any natural remedy.** As with any remedy, the misuse of natural remedies can have negative consequences for your health. The author is not a doctor or naturopath. The information in this book is for educational purposes only; it is not medical advice nor an endorsement of any particular medical or health treatment.
- **Do not disregard medical advice or delay, change, or discontinue medical treatment because of the information in this book.**

Young morel mushrooms

Contents

Introduction 9
Introduction to Using Food as Medicine 11
   Why Forage? 11

Spring 15
   Stinging Nettle 17
   Spanakopita with Wild Stinging Nettles *19*
   Wild Vegetable Curry *21*
   Nettle Pistou Buns *23*
   Japanese Knotweed 27
   Pickled Japanese Knotweed *29*
   Oyster Mushrooms 31
   Oyster Mushroom and Cheese Omelette *35*
   Fiddleheads 37
   Pickled Fiddleheads *38*
   Asian Fiddlehead Recipe *39*
   Horsetail Powder *41*
   Miner's Lettuce 43
   Wild Watercress 45
   Wild Nodding Onion 49
   Wild Onion Compound Butter *51*
   Morel Mushrooms 53
   Morel Mushroom Soup *55*
   Fir or Spruce Tree Tips 56
   Spruce or Fir Tip Simple Syrup *57*
   Common Cattail 59
   Fireweed 61
   Chickweed 63
   Elderflower Cordial *65*
   Wild Asparagus 67
   Asparagus Soup *69*
   Docks 71
   Arnica Flowers 75
   Arnica Oil *77*
   Juniper Berry 79

Springing into Summer 81
   Wild Edible Berries 83
   Wild Plum 83
   Salmonberry 84
   Thimbleberry 86
   Strawberry 88
   Huckleberry 91
   Lemon and Huckleberry Cake *93*
   Wild Blueberries 95
   Oxeye Daisy 99
   Forest Capers *101*
   Dandelions 103
   Dandelion Jelly *105*
   Wild Mint 107
   Sheep Sorrel 108
   Wild Roses 108
   Wild Hazelnuts 111
   Licorice Root Fern *113*
   Medicinal Herbs 115
   Wild Herbal Tea *121*

Fall 123
   Mushroom Bone Broth *125*
   Red-Belted Conk 127
   Turkey Tail 129
   Artist Conk 131
   Reishi 133
   Medicinal Mushrooms 133
   Chanterelle Antipasto *137*
   Mushroom Sloppy Joes *139*
   Shagy Manes 141
   Puffballs 143
   Hedgehogs 145

- *Creamy Hedgehog Mushroom Sauce* 146
- *Mushroom Powder Seasoning* 147
- Bear's Tooth Mushroom 149
- *Mushroom Jerky* 151
- Chicken of the Woods 153
- *Chicken of the woods Nuggets* 154
- Chicken of the Woods Parmesan Sandwiches 155
- Admirable Bolete (Velvet Bolete) .. 157
- King Bolete (Porcini) 159
- Second-Class Bolete Varieties 161
- Pine Mushroom or Matsutake 163
- *Pickled Mushrooms* 165
- Lobster Mushroom 166
- *Lobster Mushroom Chowder* 167

Winter 169
- Big Leaf Maples 170
- Other Trees to Tap 171
- *Maple Syrup* 173
- Seaweeds and Shellfish 175
- Winter Baking Projects 178
- *Sourdough Starter Recipe* 179
- *Sourdough Bread Recipe* 181
- *Sourdough Bagel Recipe* 183
- *Wild everything bagel topper* 185

Other Types of Foraging 187
- Moose 189
- Deer 189
- Grouse 190
- Black Bears 190
- Preserving meat 190
- Water Foraging a.k.a. Fishing 190

Gear and Equipment 193
- For The Chef 194
- For the Forager 195

A Different Perspective 199
- From the Mushroom 201
- From the Forest 203
- From the Berries 205
- From the Herbs 207

Final Note from The Author 209

About the Author 209

Golden Chanterelle Mushroom

Introduction

I wrote this book for all the new foragers out there. In it, I share my greatest passion, hobby, job, and lifestyle. I wrote it in a seasonal format to honour my mother, who requested it years ago when she learned about what I do and was interested in doing the same.

The book is designed so that you can flip to any season of the year and find valuable information on what you can harvest per season and how to preserve or cook with it.

For example, the image on the front cover shows a beautiful cutting board covered with elderflowers, Japanese knotweed shoots, big-leaf maple blossoms, and nettles, all found in the spring. No matter what season you're in, you can open this book and find recipes and wild ingredients to forage and use.

In this book, you will learn how to properly identify different edible species, sustainably harvest them, process them when you get home to your kitchen, and cook and enjoy these new wild ingredients. You will also learn different ways to preserve your wild ingredients, from dehydrating to freezing, canning, and even infusing them into salts and vinegar.

My goal is to help you build a strong home food culture by getting these new ingredients into the house, using them correctly, and becoming comfortable with them in your everyday life. In this way, you can enjoy blissful health for yourself and your family.

Each unique ingredient in this book is only available during a specific season. So waste no time. The nettles will not be here all year long, the fiddleheads will grow tall and become carcinogenic, the lettuce will wilt away in the summer heat, and the mushrooms from the fall will freeze up come winter. The forest always gives you what you need, not what you want. Start small, start with what you already know, and slowly, you will learn new plants as you come across them in your foraging. Soon, your pantry will grow with wild foods and medicines.

Get out there, put your boots on the ground, and enjoy the forest for all it has to offer. Food is medicine, a very common and true saying. You are what you eat, so eat the best food on the planet. Forage for yourself, forage for your family, and forage for your community for the sake of good health. Take your own health into your own hands and watch and feel as your body grows stronger with each meal you incorporate wild medicinal foods into. From roots, shoots, sprigs, branches, flowers, leaves, and saps, there are many types and forms of wild foods to harvest.

FORAGE & EAT WITH THE SEASONS

Intuitive cooking is the best way to cook. Use what you have in the home intuitively: a little handful of this, a little sprinkle of that, and you will be surprised by the things you can create. Cook with your gut, cook with love, and it will always taste good.

I hope you enjoy this book with its rich recipes, and start to empower your home food culture with me.

From our kitchen to yours, Happy Foraging!

With love,

Raeanna Layfield
Founder, Foraging with You
BC, Canada

Introduction to Using Food as Medicine

Who really enjoys taking supplement pills and tinctures? They are quite bitter, let's be honest, and you have to remember to take them every day. But if we treat food as medicine, we can take in all the nutrients we need from our daily meals. Minerals and vitamins are better absorbed into the body this way.

Today, we are relearning how to eat our medicine through cooking and baking with wild ingredients, the way things used to be: slow food made at home with your own hands. When you cook and eat this way, you control what goes into your body.

This book will teach you how to prepare and enjoy foraged plants and fungi right from your own home. From pickling omega-filled fiddleheads to drying nutrient-dense mushrooms for the winter months, the techniques and recipes in this book will help you enhance your home food culture.

WHY FORAGE?

Back in the day, "lifestyle diseases" weren't as prevalent in our culture as they are today. Diabetes, heart complications, stroke, and other diseases are on the rise. We have a major disconnect from our food, not just because we rarely cook these days but also because knowledge of wild and natural medicinal plants has been lost. Wild plants like fiddleheads, stinging nettles, burdocks, and wild lettuce all contain high amounts of trace minerals, vitamins, and even omega fatty acids. We would do well to consume more of them—not from bottles purchased from the vitamin aisle, but in the food we eat every day.

Nature gives us what we need, not what we want. I learned this a while ago. One day, I was disheartened because I had come home from a foraging trip with several new wild herbs but no mushrooms. But it didn't take me long to recognize that these herbs were a gift from nature, every bit as precious as those mushrooms I had hoped to find.

You see, we forget that this planet wants to take care of us. The medicine we need is actually never very far from reach; we just need to open our eyes. We also need to let our hearts lead us instead of our heads. For example, most of us have been taught that dandelions are undesirable weeds, and we regularly witness people spraying chemicals on them—when, in fact, dandelions are one of the most beneficial herbs for the human body.

This knowledge loss has also caused us to lose control of our money, as we run to the grocery store at the corner to restock our fridge with dead vegetables and fruits that have been picked weeks, if not months, before they got to you.

Foraging gives you freedom not only with nutrients but also financially. Anyone can go out foraging, bring home some food, do some light kitchen work, and enjoy it for free. You don't even need expensive foraging equipment; you can simply take any reusable bag or container along with you each day, filling it with nature's seasonal goodness.

But foraging doesn't only keep money in your pockets, it also gives you freedom in life! Trading with other foragers and farmers is a long-lost skill in our society, but it is so empowering that I would like to bring it back.

Also, when you eat wild food, you are forced to eat with the seasons (unless you preserve them). Eating with the seasons is a way to connect with the Earth. Walking in the forest, also called "forest bathing," enhances your health even more.

Being attuned to nature and its seasons is a skill that everyone needs to learn. Knowing, like the back of your hand, when certain mushrooms, herbs, or fruits are at their peak can save you time and energy in the long run. Then, you can use that time and energy to relax and do whatever it is you enjoy doing most.

That being said, when I'm processing herbs, I often remind myself, "Do what you love, and you will never work a day in your life." Processing harvests can feel as if it takes forever, but if I love what I do, it's not work. With this understanding, let's get into the main content of the book.

Ready? Let's start!

Notes: Please only take what you NEED, our forests are regularly over-harvested. We want to be sure that many generations have the same wild foods as we do. So be sure to follow the sustainable guidelines when harvesting. Spread wild seeds when you can, and reduce the spraying of chemicals and mass cuttings of trails.

Big Leaf Maple Blossoms

Spring

I started with spring because it is not only the beginning of life for the planet but a new beginning for each and every plant that comes out of the soil. Spring might arguably be my favourite season, although all the seasons are wonderfully unique. So, let's dive into the wild foods from this season.

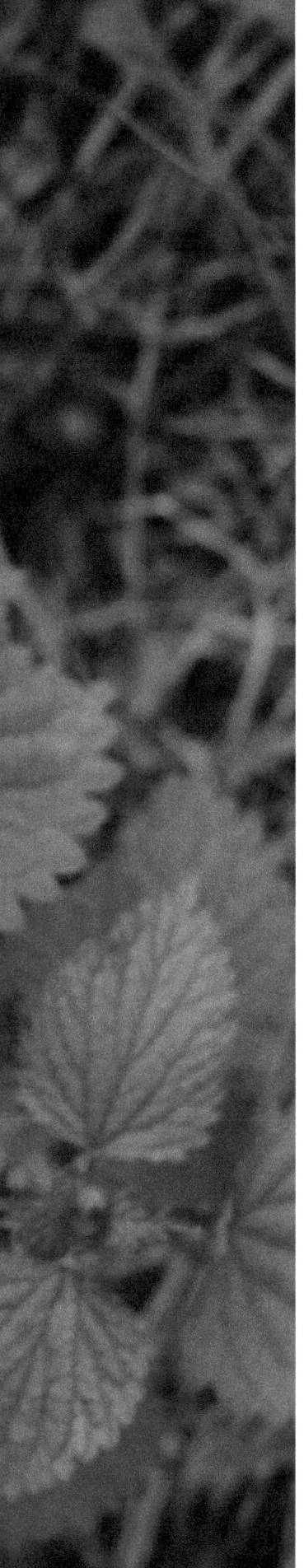

STINGING NETTLE

This plant is chlorophyll-rich, an antihistamine, and helps support your liver. In Chinese medicine, spring is liver detox season, so it is amazing that this liver-supporting herb comes up in spring just as we need it. It can also be used to heal pain in the body by stinging yourself with the leaves. High amounts of iron, magnesium, and calcium are also found in stinging nettles

Harvest: In spring to early summer, before the leaves start to droop. This plant grows almost everywhere. It likes moist ground and disturbed areas. Pick what you need, mostly the tops, with gloves. After the plant goes into seed and the leaves droop, nettles become harmful to the digestive tract. At this time, you should only use it for tea. Be sure to give your nettle patch an offering so that you can ensure more abundance in years to come. Offerings of dried tobacco, herbs, crystals, or even a piece of your hair can be given with gratitude.

Process: Wash the leaves with cool water and place them in an airtight container to store in the fridge for up to two weeks. Blanch nettles in big batches, like you would wilt spinach, and freeze them for later use. I also dehydrate my nettle leaves and store them in glass jars to use in the winter for tea or crumble on top of any meal. You can also turn them into a nutrient-dense powder to take in capsule form.

Eat: This plant can be used to make spanakopita, quiche, stir-fries, cheese dips, nettle sauces, and soups. Add dried nettles to your tea for extra Vitamin C support; we use nettles in most of the teas we serve on our tours. When wilted, the nettles can be used just like spinach.

SPANAKOPITA WITH WILD STINGING NETTLES

What you'll need:

1-pound stinging nettle leaves
4 garlic cloves
3 shallots
3 farm-fresh eggs
500g fetta or fresh cheese
1 package phyllo pastry
½ cup butter, melted

To Do:

1. Blanch the nettle leaves in boiling water and rinse with cold water. Squeeze out any remaining water and place the nettles on your chopping board. Chop them into small pieces, and place them in a bowl.
2. Sauté minced garlic cloves and shallots in a pan until caramelized. Allow this mixture to cool before adding it to the bowl.
3. Add farm-fresh eggs, cheese, a sprinkle of cayenne, salt, and pepper.
4. Unwrap your defrosted phyllo pastry, covering it with a damp cloth so it doesn't dry out as you work with each layer. Melt your butter in a saucepan, removing the white bubbles that form at the top. Use a pastry brush to brush the butter on each layer of pastry. For small triangles, I use 2 sheets of phyllo, dividing them in half and then in half again to get 4 triangles. Place your filling at the bottom of each triangle and fold corner to corner. Brush the top of each completed pastry with butter. You can then freeze these for later days or bake them in the oven at 350°F until golden brown.
5. Another option is to make a spanakopita pie. In this case, you would use a deep pie dish. Line it with 3 sheets of phyllo, place your filling inside, and add in some olives and sun-dried tomatoes. Next, fold the extra phyllo over the top of your filling, creating a top crust. Be sure to brush each layer of phyllo pastry with butter; this is what gives it that sexy, flaky texture (yes, I said sexy).

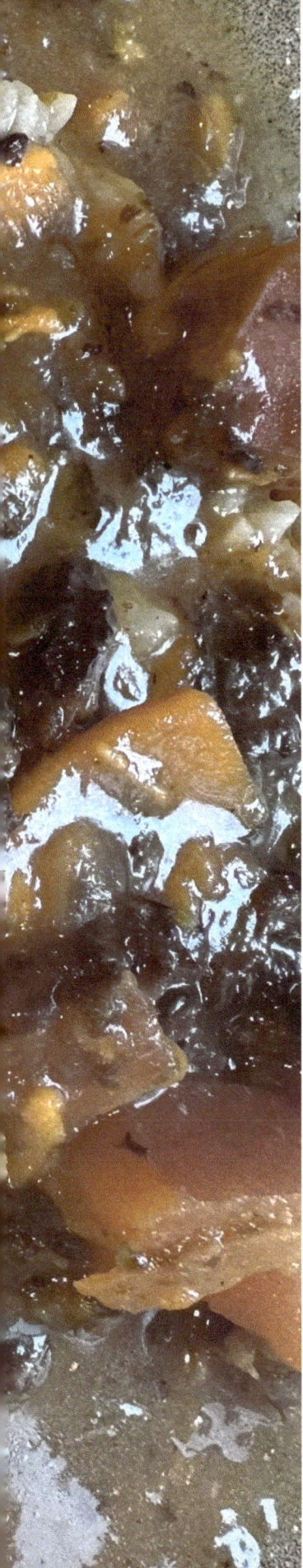

SPRING

WILD VEGETABLE CURRY

What you'll need:

1 cup cleaned fiddleheads
1 large onion, diced
2 handfuls nettles
5 knotweed shoots
1 yam
3 tablespoons curry powder
2 cans coconut milk
1 cup chickpeas
5 cloves garlic
Salt, pepper, cayenne, turmeric
1 cup chicken or turkey, optional

To Do:

1. In a large pot, sauté your onions for 5 minutes on medium heat with some oil or butter.
2. Add in your chopped nettles and fiddleheads, sautéing for another 3 minutes.
3. Add in your garlic and curry seasoning, frying the seasoning to bring out its flavour. If you're cooking with raw meat, now is the time to add it.
4. Deglaze with 2 cans of coconut milk and 2 cups of water. Add your largely diced yam and the rest of the ingredients.
5. Bring your curry to a boil, then reduce the heat to low and let it sit for 45 minutes. You will know it's finished when the yam breaks apart into the rest of the curry, making the soup a little bit thicker. Serve hot with rice and/or flatbread.

SPRING

NETTLE PISTOU BUNS

What you'll need:

1 ½ cups blanched nettles, water removed
4 garlic cloves
2 shallots
½ parmesan
¼ cup olive oil
½ sourdough bread recipe *see page 181
¼ cup sundried tomatoes, chopped
Salt and pepper

To Do:

1. To make your pistou, blend nettles, garlic, shallots, Parmesan, and olive oil together. Pistou is like pesto, but without the pine nuts. You can add nuts if you wish!
2. Roll out your dough into a perfect rectangle (this makes it easier to form buns).
3. Evenly spread your pesto onto the rectangle dough, and add in your sundried tomatoes and any other cheese you might want to add.
4. Roll the dough from the bottom up, just like cinnamon buns. Cut with a knife, or use dental floss (so the dough doesn't get squished down) about 1 ½" thick.
5. Place buns into a lightly buttered pie dish or a smaller dish, so all your buns are touching. Set aside in a warm area and cover with a damp cloth for half an hour to rise.
6. Then place the dish in the oven and bake at 350°F until golden brown (about 25 minutes).

Nettle Pistou Buns

JAPANESE KNOTWEED

The roots are known to help people with the mysterious Lyme disease, as this plant is full of resveratrol. It is also very high in minerals and tannins and can help thin blood clots.

Harvest: The shoots arrive only in early spring. Pick them at this time when they are still tender. Shoots break off easily from the base, so you can use your hand or a knife to cut them. The roots, however, are best harvested in the fall when all of the medicinal energy is in them. This plant is highly invasive, but also super medicinal. This plant looks bamboo-like, is hollow inside, and is great for forest crafts when dried from the year before.

Process: Clean the shoots by rinsing them with water. Chop them into small chunks and freeze them in a ziplock bag for later use. They can stay fresh in the fridge for a couple of days. You can also make tinctures from the roots, extracting their medicinal properties using alcohol. Take this all year round when sickness flares up.

Eat: Knotweed has a sourish taste similar to rhubarb, making it versatile for sweet or savoury dishes. Use it fresh in muffins, and vegetable stews, or pickle them with magnesium salt and vinegar for charcuterie boards. Mix with strawberries for a pie, or add to curry.

SPRING

PICKLED JAPANESE KNOTWEED

What you'll need:

6 to 8 knotweed shoots
1 cup water
1 cup apple cider vinegar
1 tablespoon kosher salt
3 dried chillies or peppercorns
3 cloves of garlic
1 tablespoon wild or domestic ginger - optional

To Do:

1. Decide if you want to pickle your knotweed in little circles or long stems, then add them into your sanitized jar. Add your garlic, chillies and any other flavours of your choice.
2. Bring all your liquid ingredients and salt to a boil, then pour over your knotweed. Seal in a canner or store unsealed with just a lid in the fridge for up to a year! You can also add about 4 tablespoons of sugar to this recipe if you like.

OYSTER MUSHROOMS

This plant is rich in amino acids, protein, vitamins, and minerals. It can greatly boost your immune system.

Harvest: In spring and summer months from dead trees that are still standing or have fallen. Cut the mushrooms from the tree, leaving unwanted pieces of the mushroom in the forest to promote healthy growth for the following season. The colour on the top is white to light brown, with white gills that smell sweet and pleasant like fruit, giving a white spore print on the paper.

Processing: Store in a paper bag or cardboard box as mushrooms need to breathe oxygen and have air circulation. Tear them by hand along the gill lines or cut with a knife. You can sauté and freeze them or dehydrate them for later use. When dehydrated, you only need to soak them in water before cooking with them.

Eat: Oyster mushrooms can be sautéed, pickled, or marinated, like other mushrooms. With a beautiful mild apricot taste, they heighten every savoury dish you add them to.

Oyster mushroom

OYSTER MUSHROOM AND CHEESE OMELETTE

What you'll need:

3 farm-fresh eggs
¼ cup smoked cheddar cheese
1 cup chopped or hand-shredded oyster mushrooms

To Do:

1. In a cast-iron pan, sauté the shredded oyster mushrooms with oil or butter. Season with salt and pepper, and remove from the pan.
2. In a bowl, whisk the eggs, a dash of cayenne, and cream if you're open to dairy—the cream makes the mixture a little more fluffy.
3. In a nonstick pan, pour a thin layer of your egg mixture, as you would a regular omelette. Then sprinkle in the cheese and oyster mushrooms. Garnish with fresh parsley or chives.

FIDDLEHEADS

Foragers hunt 2 varieties of this plant: ostrich ferns and lady ferns. Both are full of minerals, vitamins, omega-6 fatty acids, and omega-3. This nutritious vegetable will amp up your kitchen, and deepen your health and vitality.

Harvest: In the spring to early summer, before the leaves open up and they become toxic. Yes, as the leaves open and absorb sunlight, they become non-edible, so it is very important to only harvest fiddleheads in the spring while they are young and still tightly curled.

Processing: Use your fingers to rub off the little brown hairs on the fiddleheads to clean them. These hairs are edible, but they don't look appealing. To clean large amounts, place them in a draining basket and spray them all at once with a strong garden hose on high pressure. Then you can blanch and freeze them like other veggies for later use or pickle them for charcuterie boards.

Eat: Always cook fiddleheads, even if it's just for 60 seconds. If eaten raw, they are carcinogenic. Start by blanching in salted water to remove any bitter flavours, then sauté in garlic butter as a steak topper or side dish. You can also chop them up and add to your chillies, stews and stir-fry. I also pickle my fiddleheads with spruce tip-infused vinegar. This makes an amazingly bright, uplifting, tangy, and crunchy product.

PICKLED FIDDLEHEADS

What you'll need:

2 cups fiddleheads
¾ cup vinegar
¾ cup water
½ cup cane sugar
1 tablespoon pickling salt
1 clove garlic
1 tablespoon dill (optional)

To Do:

1. Blanch freshly picked and cleaned fiddleheads, then cool right away with cold running water or an ice bath.
2. For the pickling mixture, add ¾ cup of vinegar, ½ cup of sugar, and a tablespoon of salt to ¾ cup of water to a pot, bringing to a boil. You may also add aromatics like, pepper, and chillies if desired. Pour over fiddleheads, then store in the fridge for 5 days before testing them out. Use spruce tip vinegar if desired.

ASIAN FIDDLEHEAD RECIPE

What you'll need:

2 cups cleaned fiddleheads
3 tablespoons crunchy peanut butter
1 tablespoon soy sauce
1 teaspoon sugar
3 to 4 teaspoons water
½ teaspoon chillies (optional)

To Do:

1. In a large pot of salted boiling water, cook your fiddleheads for 4 minutes until they are just tender. Then cool them quickly in an ice bath and cold running water so they keep their crunch and do not overcook.
2. In a medium bowl, whisk the remaining ingredients together.
3. Add the fiddleheads to the mixture and toss gently. Garnish with some shredded carrots or peanuts, and serve at room temperature.

HORSETAIL

This plant is full of silica, helping you form collagen in the body to strengthen your joints, ligaments, and tendons, and renew the skin. It is used for mending fractured bones, sprains, and rheumatism, as well as treating and preventing osteoporosis. It also helps with urination for bladder or urinary tract infections, and with kidney stones. Antioxidant-rich, this plant grows in moist places abundantly. Plants are great at resembling what they do in the human body – this plant breaks apart into little puzzle pieces, like joints in our body, which is why it's also called the puzzle plant.

Harvest: Horsetail shoots first come up in spring but can also appear in summer months after the rains. Pick them only when they are young and the leaves are not drooping. Drooping leaves indicate an older plant with no nutrients left. There are male and female horsetails in the wild, both of which are edible.

Process: If picked young and fresh, they can be pickled or stored in the fridge to eat fresh. You can also dehydrate them in a dehydrator or dry them 100% under the sun. Then blend the horsetail into a fine green, nutrient-rich powder. Capsule the powder for a supplement pill or add it to cookies, smoothies, or cakes.

Eat: Steam young shoots lightly, then sauté in garlic and butter. Chop and add to stews, chillies, or pizza! Garnish salads with young horsetail plants as they naturally pull apart like a puzzle-looking like a star, a beautiful addition to any dish. I will also add the dried plant to herbal tea mixtures.

SPRING

HORSETAIL POWDER

What you'll need:

Horsetail plants, not including the root

To Do:

1. Cut off the root from the horsetail and dehydrate the plant until 100% dry.
2. Once dry, place the plants into a blender, blending on medium speed until you get a fine powder. You can then transfer the powder into little gel caps from the health food store or sprinkle it on smoothies, cookies, stews, or other foods of your choice.
3. Store in a glass jar in your cupboard for easy use.

MINER'S LETTUCE

Like most lettuces, miner's lettuce is full of protein, vitamins C and A, beta-carotene, and iron. Because it comes from the forest, a nutrient-dense soil, it has more of the above benefits than store-bought lettuce, which is usually now grown hydroponically with additives. This plant gets its name from the olden-day mine workers. As they worked in the mines all winter long, they looked forward to the first lettuces of spring full of Vitamin C.

Harvest: In spring, when it is the most abundant, during the moist summer, and even early in the fall when the rain returns. It grows on the sides of trails, on the forest floor, and often on the sides of parks. Cut half or most of the stems from the plant, but leave the root in the ground to ensure its continued sustainable growth.

Process: This wild lettuce makes for a juicy trail snack; sometimes, I just sit on the ground pondering what to harvest as I munch on some crunchy miner's lettuce. All you need to do with this plant is rinse it lightly and enjoy it fresh within 2 to 3 days of harvesting. You can also store it on a damp piece of paper towel in the refrigerator, sealed in a container. Consume within 3 days of harvesting.

Eat: Miner's lettuce is very mild in flavour compared to the watercress family, making it a versatile green for any dish. You can use it as a topping for stir-fries or pho with its thick, crispy stems that act like bean sprouts. Use the stems and soft leaves for fresh salad mixes, wraps, or sandwiches.

WILD WATERCRESS

Watercress is jam-packed with antioxidants and vitamin C, which helps support the body's immune system and collagen growth.

Harvest: In the spring, after the winter frosts have passed, and then into the summer. It grows in slow-moving streams that aren't affected by rising and declining rivers. When harvesting, use scissors and clip the top, leaving the roots behind so the plant can continue growing. Closely related is the Hairy Bittercress; the branches of this small herb all grow out from the centre with rounded leaves on the stems. It is similar in taste, a little darker, and has a white flower when it grows older.

Process: Bacteria and E. coli are often found in streams located below cattle farms or beaver dams, so be sure to wash well with some vinegar and lots of fresh water.

Eat: Watercress has a peppery or spicy flavour. Enjoy this wild lettuce on a burger or mixed with other wild greens in a salad. It stays crisp and dark green when stored airtight in the refrigerator for up to a week. It also works great for sandwiches and wraps, adding that nice peppery zing. You can also add it to any pesto recipe for an extra punch of radish flavour.

Watercress Salad

WILD NODDING ONION

The juice from wild onions can be used to treat sore throats, kidney stones, colds, and fevers. Dry this plant and use it as a poultice (herbal press) for any respiratory issues that may arise.

Harvest: In the spring, as they go to seed in the summer, which makes them harder to process with the flowering stem. Wild onions are found on the sides of lakes and rivers. They are a special plant and should be harvested with great care, taking only what you need. To harvest, dig down with your finger or a knife, wiggle and pull up to remove the whole root system and reveal the small whitish-pink bulb. The tops of the onions are clearly visible, standing like thick strands of green grass.

Process: Peel away some of the outside layers to reveal the crisp white-pink fleshy bulb before washing. If I am picking them near a stream, I will rinse them in the running water to remove any extra dirt before bringing them home.

Eat: Grill your wild onions whole over the fire or BBQ, like traditionally done by our First Nations people. Chop them to add to your favourite dish, like regular green onions, or wrap them in a paper towel and store them fresh in your fridge for up to a week, ensuring the roots are kept damp. Slice and dehydrate them to make dried onion flakes for your pantry, compound butter, or poultices

WILD ONION COMPOUND BUTTER

What you'll need:

1 pound butter at room temperature
4 tablespoons crushed dry nettle
4 tablespoons dried wild onions
½ teaspoon salt
¼ teaspoon smoked black pepper
Dash of cayenne pepper

To Do:

1. Whip butter with an electric mixer until it is light in colour and fluffy, then add all the other ingredients and whip again.
2. Store in the fridge for up to 2 weeks, or roll in parchment paper and freeze until needed for a steak topper or to cook with.

Notes: We regularly serve this wild herb butter on fresh sourdough during our spring and summer foraging tours. Our guests always enjoy it, plus the pink from the onion marbles shines through the white butter, making it quite appealing.

MOREL MUSHROOMS

Morels are full of vitamin D, support immune functions in the body, and have antioxidant and antibacterial properties. They also contain minerals such as copper and iron and are a great source of fibre and zinc.

Harvest: In the spring, when temperatures reach 17°F to 20°F. You will find various colours of edible morels, like the burnsite morel, the natural morel, and the blond morels. The burnsite morel grows abundantly after forest fires. It is the first mushroom to appear after a fire, absorbing nutrients from the burned forest floor. It can appear up to 2 years after a forest fire, with the highest production in the first year. Its cap has concave patterns with no gills, and it attaches directly to the white stem. Both the cap and stem are hollow inside when cut open; this is how to know it's a true morel. The poisonous look-alikes will not be hollow inside, nor are they beautiful to the eye.

Process: Unless covered in ash, there is no need to wash them. If you wish to remove bugs that may be present, soak them in cold, salted water. To preserve, dehydrate them completely and store them in a glass jar or vacuum-sealed bag for up to 3 years. It is believed that the longer they are stored, the more flavorful they become, especially with their smoky essence. These mushrooms have a firm and meaty texture, so they can be pre-sautéed and then frozen in small portions for later use.

Eat: Large morels can be stuffed with meat or rice mixtures, then slowly sautéed or roasted in the oven. Dry them first, then soak them so their flesh is strong enough to hold the stuffing. They can also be chopped into small pieces and sautéed to have a texture similar to ground beef, making them a great meat substitute. Slicing them into rings is also enjoyable due to their hollow inside. My favourite recipe with my first morel harvest is the morel cream sauce below, which you can make with fresh or dried mushrooms. It is very important to always cook this mushroom before eating! Also, be careful when consuming them with alcohol; this may change the effect they have on your body. Everyone reacts differently to wild mushrooms, try small amounts if it's your first time.

MOREL CREAM SAUCE

What you'll need:

2 cups fresh morels or 1 cup dried morels, soaked in water
3 cloves garlic, minced
2 shallots, minced
1 litre heavy cream 35%
1 tablespoon butter
2 tablespoons parmesan cheese
Fresh herbs, such as thyme and sage, chopped

To Do:

1. In a sauté pan, start to sauté your mushrooms with butter or olive oil. You want to make sure your pan has sides, as we are making the sauce in this pan as well.
2. After 5 minutes, add in your minced shallots. Cook for 2 minutes, then add your minced garlic, making sure not to burn it.
3. Pour in all your heavy cream and reduce the heat to a low simmer, tussling the pan occasionally as the cream reduces and thickens.
4. Add the butter and parmesan cheese. Add the chopped fresh herbs and cook for one more minute. Serve hot with pasta or simply dip bread into this sauce.

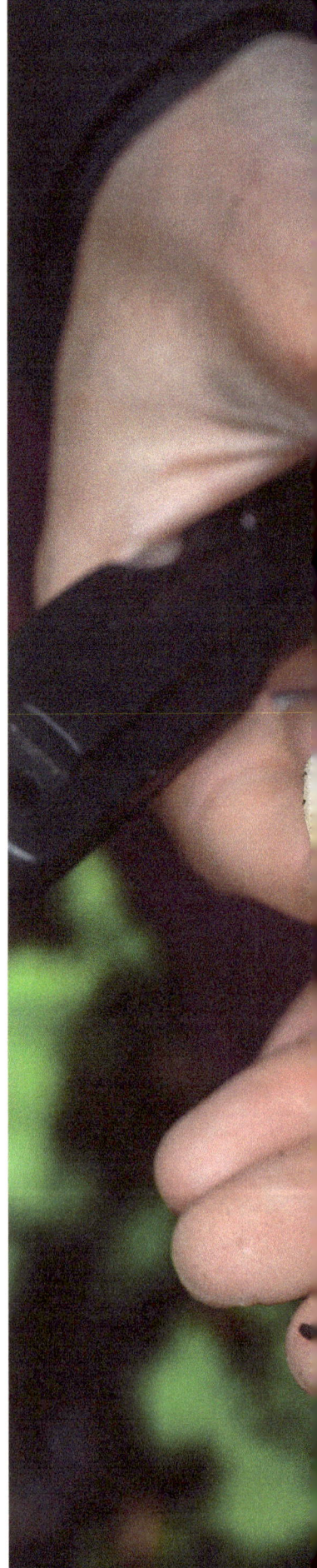

SPRING

MOREL MUSHROOM SOUP

What you'll need:

2 cups fresh morels or 1 cup dried morels, soaked
1 large onion
4 stalks celery
5 cloves garlic
1 bay leaf
4 cans coconut milk or regular milk

To Do:

1. If you're using dried morels, soak them in cold water for 10 minutes before starting your soup. Chop your onion and celery—larger pieces are okay for all of this because we will be blending the soup at the end. Add them to a large soup pot and sauté with butter or oil for 6 minutes.
2. Remove the morels from the water, squeezing out excess water. Then chop them roughly and add them to the pot.
3. Once everything looks cooked and smells delicious, add your garlic and cook for a few more minutes, stirring often to prevent the garlic from burning, as this will give it a bitter taste.
4. Add the coconut milk, 2 cups of water, bay leaf, salt, pepper, and a little bit of cayenne. Simmer for 30 minutes.
5. Turn off the heat and allow the soup to cool before blending it thoroughly.
6. Once everything is blended, add it back to your pot and simmer lightly for 10 minutes. Garnish with wild onion tops and croutons if you wish.

FORAGE & EAT WITH THE SEASONS

FIR OR SPRUCE TREE TIPS

Coniferous tree tips (needled trees, not leafy trees) contain high levels of vitamins C, A, and E and are a natural expectorant for coughs. They also contain magnesium and potassium.

Harvest: In spring to summer, when they grow their fresh tips that eventually make the trees bigger. Collect just the fresh tips of the trees. Each tree will have a unique flavour, so taste to see what you like best before collecting a whole bunch.

Process: No washing or much work is needed after harvesting. I pick my tips directly into a bag with small holes (as I do with many wild herbs that I dry) so that they can start to dry right away. Harvesting into a plastic bag works too, but they will start to build condensation after a short while.

Eat: Add fresh tree tips to plain white vinegar and infuse for 2-3 months. Then strain and add to your salad dressings or pickled vegetables. They are also great for making simple syrup. I also use them in my wild tea blends; their lemony flavour is very uplifting, making it a wonderful cold tea drink for the summer months. Blend your tree tips with salts or sugars to infuse and preserve the flavour. I also freeze them for later use in my baked goods or on top of salmon.

SPRUCE OR FIR TIP SIMPLE SYRUP

What you'll need:

1 cup tree tips
2 cups sugar
2 cups water

To Do:

1. Add water and sugar to a pot and simmer until the sugar is dissolved. Set aside to cool slightly before adding the tree tips.
2. Allow to infuse for 2 hours, then strain and enjoy with teas, cocktails, or mocktails. Also great drizzled over desserts.

COMMON CATTAIL

Cattail helps prevent anemia, has antiseptic properties, and can help control diabetes. It also contains vitamins K and B6, magnesium, fibre, and iron.

Harvest: In the spring when the shoots just start sprouting from the ground. The taste is light like cucumber, and is very refreshing. Pull them from the ground of a clean pond or swamp, away from railroads, highways, or cow farms.

Process: Peel away the tougher outer layers of the shoots to get the soft, light green, juicy insides. You can also harvest and grind the roots into nutrient-dense flour by pounding them in water, and then straining and drying them. Grind the ripe cattail heads and use them as a thickening and binding agent, similar to flour; they are rich in protein. This is a great gluten-free option.

Eat: Enjoy the young shoots on the spot, pickle them, or store them in your fridge for several days. Use them in salads, and sushi rolls, or finish your stir-fries with them. They could resemble bamboo shoots when used this way.

FIREWEED

Fireweed contains vitamins A, C, and D, Calcium, and potassium. It is used for pain and swelling, fevers, tumours, wounds, and an enlarged prostate. High levels of tannins make fireweed astringent, improving and toning the colon and digestive system. As it is antifungal, it can help with candida overgrowth (yeast) in the intestines. The summer leaves can be used as tea for sore throats or lung congestion. The roots are also used for medicinal tincture making.

Harvest: In the spring, when the shoots are nice and tender and before the leaves open up too much and start to get bitter—simply break them off at the base. They usually grow in abundance in logging blocks, on the sides of dirt roads, and after fires. Although the leaves turn bitter in summer, this plant is edible all year round. In summer, its purple flowers appear, which are wonderful for garnishing salads or cakes.

Process: There is not much to do; just rinse well. As you pick them, place them all the same way for easy washing. When the plant grows tall in the summer, pinch at the top with one hand as the other glides down, harvesting the long leaves.

Eat: I often blend young fireweed shoots into my smoothie, giving it a light lemony flavour. You can also grill them whole, season with salt, pepper, and olive oil, or chop them up and add them to a salad. You can also pickle them. I also love harvesting their flowers in the summer to decorate cupcakes, lemonades, or just to use as an edible flower arrangement for the table.

CHICKWEED

This plant is very good for digestion and for eczema when applied topically. It is rich in vitamins and phytonutrients, and acts as a body tonic that boosts the immune system.

Harvest: In the spring and summer. Chickweed can be found in gardens with its little white flowers and hairy stems. Use a pair of scissors or pinch them off by hand to harvest, making sure to keep them clean as you go. This plant is one of the most abundant wild lettuces that most people overlook. I have even found it growing during mild winter months with all the rain. It is usually weeded out of the garden, but I prefer to leave it and harvest it as the digestion support is much better than that of cultivated lettuces.

Process: Rinse with cold water, dry, and then store them on a paper towel in a sealed container or bag in the fridge. You can dry and blend it into powder to take as a supplement or to add to your baking recipe during the winter months.

Eat: You can enjoy chickweed right away. Its crunchy texture works like sprouts in sandwiches and wraps, and it makes a great addition to any salad mix.

ELDERFLOWERS

Elderflower pollen boosts the immune system and helps with seasonal allergies. They are antibacterial and antiviral and help expel toxins from the body. The stems and leaves of the elderberry plant are poisonous. Only the dark purple berries are medicinal and edible, not the red ones from the Sambucus racemosa var. variety. Flowers from both plants are good to use.

Harvest: The window to harvest elderflowers is very short, I mean very. I pay particular attention to areas closer to town and then work my way up to the mountain, where they bloom later. When the elderberry bush blooms, it produces a cluster of very small, cream-coloured flowers. You can see the little clusters through the green forests from quite a distance. Gather them into a clean bowl to keep the pollen that falls off them. The stems, leaves, and bark of this plant are NOT edible.

Process: Remove the little flowers from the stems using a fork, making sure to keep the pollen. You can store the flowers in the fridge for up to 3 days. They can also be dried and used as tea when one is sick with a fever. Elderflowers are very gentle and safe for children.

Eat: A great way to preserve this beautiful floral essence is by making an elderflower cordial. They also go well infused into baked custards like creme brulee, and puddings, and, of course, can be used for garnishing. Elderflowers can also be used for fermenting, thanks to the natural yeast in the pollen. Make a strong elderflower tea with hot water, honey and lemon. Place it in the freezer, stirring every 45 minutes, to make a frozen dessert called granita. This is super refreshing during the hot summer months.

ELDERFLOWER CORDIAL

What you'll need:

400g elderflowers
4 ½ cups honey
2 litres pre-boiled water
2-3 lemons, juice and zest
50g citric acid

To Do:

1. Grate your lemons using a hand grater and transfer them into a large bowl, then add the elderflowers that have had the stems removed (adding stems will make it bitter).
2. Juice your lemons and add the juice to the bowl, then add the citric acid. The citric acid is optional, but it will make the recipe last longer in your fridge.
3. Add hot water and honey. Mix well, and let it sit for 2 hours. Then, strain well into a clean storage jar. Store in the refrigerator for up to one month.

WILD ASPARAGUS

Asparagus contains all the regular vitamins and minerals and is a great source of fibre, protein, and carbohydrates. However, it is most high in vitamins K and folate. It is also full of water, making it hydrating for the body. You will never forget you have eaten asparagus because, as soon as you go to the washroom, you will be quickly reminded of its essence. For some reason, this brings a smile to my face when I remember it.

Harvest: In spring, when the shoots start to poke out from the ground and are anywhere from 6-10 inches tall. Asparagi is the young shoot of the plant before it flowers in the summer. The harvest window lasts about a month. You can find them along riverbanks, especially at the point where the river goes into the ocean; that's where I have found white asparagus. They are also popular along railroads, as the workers back in the day planted them for food. I have found some on Vancouver Island, but mostly in the interior of BC. When harvesting, snap off the asparagus where it easily breaks. If they are taller (you arrived late in the season), don't go down too far, as they can get woody, making them very unpleasant to consume.

Process: Asparagus is great pickled or eaten fresh. It can be stored in the fridge for up to 2 weeks and can also be cut into small pieces and dehydrated for winter soups. You only need to rinse them and enjoy!

Eat: One of the first things I make with my asparagus harvest, besides eating them raw and fresh, is cream of asparagus soup. This soup is coconut milk-based, and tastes best when cooked over the fire and combined with wild onions. Pickled asparagus can be enjoyed in Caesar salad, with charcuterie boards, or on its own. Grilling them lightly on the BBQ along with a steak is also another popular option.

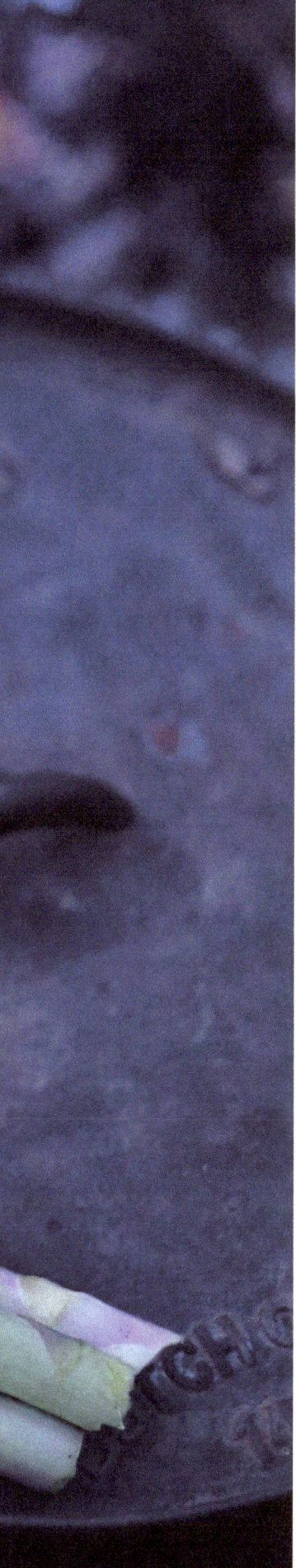

SPRING

ASPARAGUS SOUP

What you'll need:

1 pound wild asparagus
2 cans coconut milk
1 cup chopped wild onions or regular white onions
2 cloves garlic or wild garlic
2 dashes worcestershire sauce
Cayenne
Pepper
Salt

To Do:

1. Start by sautéing your onions in a large pot with oil or butter until translucent and soft. Then add your garlic and chopped asparagus, sautéing for a few minutes to get the flavours out.
2. Add your coconut milk and 1 cup of water. Allow to simmer for 20 minutes.
3. Season to taste, and serve hot. Cooking over a campfire will add a beautiful, smoky flavour. You can also puree this soup if children don't like the chunks of veggies.

69

Yellow Dock

DOCKS

The plants in the dock family are a good source of potassium, calcium, and amino acids. They aid in digestion and inflammation, whether used topically or internally.

Harvest: In early spring, before they get too bitter. Docks are a family of green plants that, when young, grow low to the ground and spread their spade-shaped leaves out from one center point. The leaves, stems, and roots of docks can be eaten for medicine or used in the kitchen as a vegetable. Burdock leaves are dark green, thin, and attached to a juicy, thick stem like Swiss chard. Burdock is prized for its taproot, which is white to cream in colour and can be up to 2 feet long. In Japan, burdock root is called Gobo.

Yellow dock leaves appear waxy and have red veins running through them. Yellow dock root tastes bitter and is used as medicine. It is bright yellow, similar in colour to turmeric. You can make yourself a bitter tincture out of yellow dock root, or dry the root to add to your tea when you need some more digestive support. An old saying goes, "Bitter to the tongue, sweet to your liver," and many other organs, I might add. I try to use bitters daily for my digestion and gallbladder, as suggested by many naturopaths I have met in my studies.

Process: Soak and rinse dock roots well with water to remove dirt. Store burdock roots fresh for one week in the fridge, or dehydrate and store in a glass jar. Make yourself an alcohol tincture using the folk method, so you don't folk it up! That is, fill a jar one-half to three-quarters full of plant matter, then fill the rest with liquid.

Eat: Steam/simmer burdock root until tender. Cool, then slice thinly and dress with sesame seeds, soy, some vinegar, green onions, and chilis. You can also add the steamed root to mashed potatoes or stir-fries. When enjoying the leaves as raw or cooked green, remember they are spring green, so they will have a slightly bitter taste to help detox the liver and body during this natural detox time for the planet. Just add a little to your salads vs. only making a salad from them.

Burdock

Clean by scrapping the yellow dock root

ARNICA FLOWERS

Arnica is a widely used medicinal flower for bruises, sprains and strains. Arnica is **not edible.** Do not consume orally. Use it only topically to heal the body of pain or to treat injuries.

Harvest: In spring, that is the only time it will grow. It has bright yellow petals like daisies, a yellow centre, and a green stem with 2 to 4 pointy green leaves. Pick just the flowers to infuse into oils. Your hands will smell beautiful afterwards, by the way. Arnica is often found at higher elevations in BC, especially towards the mountains and the interior, where you find some of the wild sage. You will see this beautiful yellow flower in abundance around Merritt, Kamloops, Williams Lake and up to Smithers and Terrace. I've been making the below oil infusion for years; it was the first flower medicine I ever worked with. I use it to treat my whole family, including my in-laws. Now I even have massage therapist using it to help with their recovery from overworking and to provide healing benefits to their clients.

Process: Air dry for half a day, then promptly infuse them into organic oils of your choice. I like to use half coconut oil and half olive oil so that the mixture is hard when kept at room temperature. You cannot dry arnica flowers to use later, as they will turn into fluff like dandelions do. Use the folk method so you don't folk it up - just kidding. Making oil infusions is very easy; just be sure your flowers or plant matter is always fully covered with oil so they don't oxidise and go bad (you can smell this).

ARNICA OIL

What you'll need:

1 large mason jar filled ¾ of the way with half-dried arnica flowers
1 ½ cups organic olive oil
1 ½ cups coconut oil
2 tablespoons vitamin E in liquid form

To Do:

1. Before adding your flowers to the jar, smush and bruise them with your hands to release their healing oils. Then fill the jar with your oils of choice, stirring and tussling the mixture around.
2. Push all the flowers under the oil, placing a weight on top to keep them submerged.
3. Cover your jar with a cloth so the mixture can breathe (important). Label the jar "For topical use only," then store it in a dark place for one month. Oils will go rancid if stored in light, so you can cover your jar with a brown paper bag if it's near light. To help the infusion along, stir after two weeks.
4. After a month or so, strain well and add the vitamin E. Mix well and divide into smaller jars for storage and use. You can use it right away, remembering only to apply it topically. See our YouTube channel, Foraging with You, for tutorial videos.

Reminder: Arnica flowers cannot be consumed orally. Use only topically for healing. Label the jar accordingly.

JUNIPER BERRY

These berries aid in digestion, stimulate appetite, relieve colic and water retention, and treat diarrhea. They also help with bladder health. Clients of mine have told me that juniper berries taken as a tea or tincture worked great for their bladder infections.

Harvest: Juniper is a low evergreen shrub in the cypress family. I often find it at higher elevations alongside my arnica flower harvests. Juniper berries take 5 years to ripen from their green state to a dark purple berry. They are not a juice-filled berry you would use for smoothies and pies, but more of a dry, seed-like berry. These berries are widely known for flavouring and making gin, beer, and other alcoholic drinks. Harvest only the dark purple berries; this means they are ripe. Leave the green ones for another time.

Process: The berries are usually dry by the time you harvest them. Simply continue the drying process, then store them in an airtight container.

Eat: Juniper berries are a great flavouring spice for wild game or lamb. The strong flavour of these meats pairs nicely with the strong flavour of the berry. I simply blend my juniper berries with salt to infuse the salt with juniper essence. Make this infusion as strong or as mild as you would like, intuitively cooking with your senses. Sprinkle your infused salt onto your steaks or roasts before cooking for a well-balanced overall flavour.

Springing into Summer

This chapter has a funny name because many of the flowers and other plants here start to grow in the spring when they can be identified, but their fruit or herbal parts are not available until summer. So this is our summer section. Enjoy!

WILD EDIBLE BERRIES

Caution note: When harvesting any berries, remember that you are not the only one in the forest eating them. Bears are almost always around, and rely on these berries as a food source before their winter hibernation. Use a bear bell to make lots of noise, or find comfort harvesting with a canine while your head is in the bushes. Be sure to always leave some for the squirrels and birds as well.

WILD PLUM

As the fruit hangs from the shrub/tree, so do the little white flowers in spring. You can expect dark purple little plums to ripen and hang from the branches by mid-summer. They are just like regular plums with a single pit inside, but smaller, making them great for hiking snacks. They can be used to make jam or compote, stewing them until a paste forms. Strain out the pits and you can use the flesh for an Asian plum sauce or sweet jam for toast. The flavour is a little musky, and might not be for everyone, but once blended with a sweetener, it makes a great dip for chicken nuggets or fried prawns.

Flowering Salmonberry

SALMONBERRY

The salmonberry is the <u>first</u> berry flower to arrive in the spring. It looks quite similar to a wild rose, with pink petals gracing you on your early spring walks. You can collect the flower petals to decorate early spring cakes or garnish salads. Shortly after the flower petals fall off, the middle of the bud turns into a fruiting body called the berry. Resembling salmon roe, this berry's red or pale orange colour does not indicate its ripeness. You can only test the ripeness by checking the berry's resistance when you pull it from the branch. Salmonberries are very fragile and can be picked directly onto a paper towel in a container or in a flat cardboard box. They can be used to make jam, jelly, or to flavour wild game sauce. They are also great for making scones and muffins.

Salmonberry

Flowering Thimbleberry

THIMBLEBERRY

The thimbleberry is the <u>second</u> berry to arrive in the forest for harvesting. The flower is large and white, and the leaves look similar to those of raspberry leaves in our gardens. This berry starts off white, then turns a deep red with lots of little seeds. It is shaped like a dome or iglu. This berry is very fragile to harvest, and is often eaten as a trail snack. I however pick them directly into small Ziploc bags, which I then throw in the freezer for smoothies or jams. The leaves are a wonderful source of vitamin C. They can be dried for tea or even used to wrap your berries in as you walk or if you have forgotten a bag.

Thimbleberry

Flowering Strawberry

STRAWBERRY

Wild strawberries yield a small white flower in spring and give their berry in summer. Its 3 oval leaves make it look similar to the garden strawberry, but smaller. You can eat them right off the bush, or gather them in a small carton. A recipe from when I was five years old is to smash the berries instantly into jam for toast. But the older me would say to use them fresh in a spring spinach salad with goat cheese and a balsamic dressing. When camping, they are a great addition to pancakes.

Strawberry

HUCKLEBERRY

Harvested around August, the red huckleberry is the <u>last</u> berry to become ready for consumption. You can find them abundantly in the lower mainland of BC, Canada, and all over Vancouver Island. They grow to about your shoulder and head height, unlike the low-bush dark huckleberries found in the alpines; they are a low bush. This berry is great for muffins, frozen yogurts, compotes, and smoothies. The huckleberry flowers are shaped like little fairy bells that hang from the small shrub branches. Do not harvest the flowers because it would prevent the berry from forming. Once the berries are out, the fastest way to harvest them is with a bucket or bag tied to a rope around your neck so you can use two hands

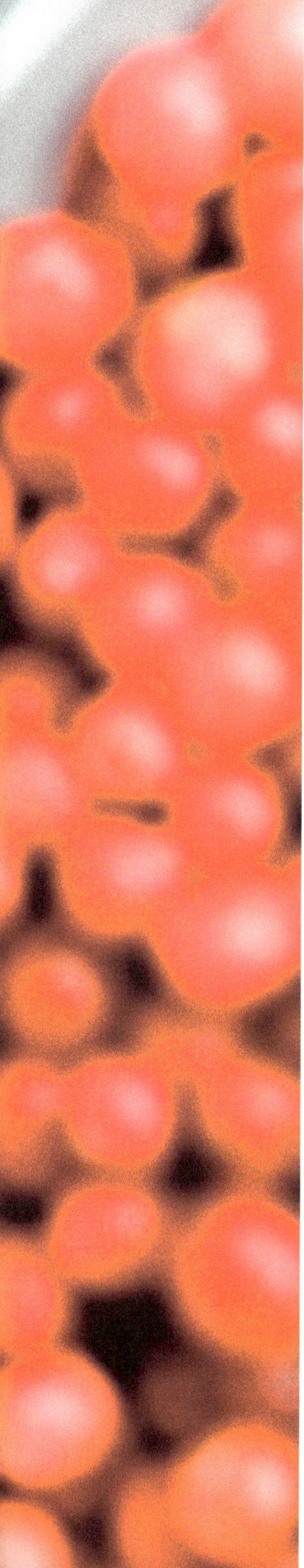

SPRINGING INTO SUMMER

LEMON AND HUCKLEBERRY CAKE

What you'll need:

½ cup butter
1 cup sugar
2 eggs
1 lemon, juiced and zested
1 ½ cups flour
1 teaspoon baking powder
1 teaspoon salt
2 teaspoons vanilla
¼ cup cream or nut milk
1 cup wild huckleberries

To Do:

1. Whip butter and sugar in a large bowl until fluffy and white. Then mix in the eggs one at a time, followed by half the lemon juice and all of the lemon zest.
2. Mix the remaining ingredients in a different bowl and then add the mixture to the first bowl. Mix until just combined.
3. Bake in the oven for 20 minutes at 350°F, testing for doneness with a toothpick.
4. Optional icing: Mix 5 tablespoons of icing sugar and the remaining lemon juice. and zest. Pour over the cake while still slightly warm. Cool and serve.

WILD BLUEBERRIES

Wild blueberries are a deep purple when ripe. The leaves are oval-shaped, tough, and green. High-bush blueberries are just a little smaller than your regular grocery store blueberries. Wild low-bush blueberries are very small and are found in higher elevations; I have found them in northern British Columbia. They are delicious and full of antioxidants. Canadian foragers ship them over to China for a fair dollar, where they are used as an anti-cancer agent. Dehydrate the berries for teas, or stew them and make jams, jellies, and pies. I usually freeze mine in bags and pull them out for muffins, scones, and cakes as needed.

SALAL

The berries from the salal bush create a dark purple berry cluster, the highest berry in pectin. They are great for making jams or jellies without the gelatin. While they are not the sweetest or smoothest textured berries in the forest, they are packed with many antioxidants and vitamins. Salal branches and leaves are collected for florists to use in bouquets.

OREGON GRAPE

A prickly Holly look-alike, you see this plant on many hikes in BC. The leaves are mostly green with red and yellow appearances during the summer and fall. In spring, it blossoms a yellow cluster of edible flowers that are crunchy like popcorn, and have a sweet and sour taste. After the yellow flowers bloom, juicy green berries form and grow until they turn dark purple. I pick the berries when they are still green, and pickle them to make forest capers.

OXEYE DAISY

This plant is used to treat common colds, coughs, bronchitis, liver and gallbladder complaints, loss of appetite, and fluid retention. It is high in vitamins A and C, beta-carotene, and riboflavin. Its mature leaves were traditionally used as insect repellent.

Harvest: Oxeye daisies are a common wildflower abundant in fields and along roadsides. It has many white petals and a yellow center, with uneven rounded dark green leaves. If you can identify the green leaves before the flower stems sprout, they make a great salad addition and are very pleasant in flavour. You can also collect the unopened flowering buds to use as pickled forest capers before the small daisy buds open (use the prior recipe for this).

Process: Keep the closed daisy buds organized and separated from the opened flowers so you can pickle them (not bitter at all compared to the Oregon grape berries)

Eat: Pickle the closed daisy buds and use them just like capers. We call these forest capers; they have a beautiful taste. You can dry the open flowers and use them for nutritious tea mixes or to decorate desserts. My husband made me pancakes with daisy flowers and wild strawberries cooked into them once. It's such a delight to enjoy flowers with food; they bring beauty and elegance into any salad or cake

FOREST CAPERS

What you'll need:

1 cup green Oregon grape berries or daisy buds
½ cup white vinegar
½ cup water
2 teaspoons salt
1 teaspoon ground pepper or 1 whole red chilli
1 bay leaf

To Do:

1. Wash your berries well, then strain. Place them into a sanitized medium mason jar.
2. Bring your liquids to a boil, and add the salt, pepper and bay leaf.
3. Pour the mixture over the berries, seal and store in the fridge for 1 week before tasting them. I like to use these best when making tartar sauce for my wild salmon or fish fries with friends.

SPRINGING INTO SUMMER

DANDELIONS

A heart and liver-supporting herb, dandelion can help reduce cholesterol, balance blood sugar levels, reduce inflammation, reduce blood pressure, and aid in weight loss, all while supporting the immune system, of course.

Harvest: Dandelion roots are best gathered in early spring or fall. All of the energy is in the roots during these times, making them larger as well. The plant's young leaves are less bitter in the spring and can be used in salads, while the flower tops are harvested in the spring through summer.

Process: Harvest the leaves and flowers separately so you don't have to organize them when you get home. Allow time for the bugs to leave the flowers before using them. Wash the roots well before bringing them into the kitchen.

Eat: Use the roots as a coffee substitute by roasting them in the oven, and blending them into powder. The flower tops can be dipped into a tempura batter, (leaving the stem attached), deep-fried, and finished with a little bit of icing sugar for a fun dessert. Make beautiful dandelion jelly from the flowers. The green leaves are great to eat in a salad; be sure to mix them in with some other wild lettuce as they are slightly bitter.

Dandelion Jelly on Sourdough

SPRINGING INTO SUMMER

DANDELION JELLY

What you'll need:

4 cups dandelion petals, lightly packed
4 cups sugar (I like organic cane sugar or honey)
2 tablespoons lemon juice
3.5 tablespoons pectin
4 cups water

To Do:

1. After you have harvested your dandelion flowers, sit down and remove the yellow pedals from the green base, so you are not using any green bits to make this jelly.
2. Boil 4 cups of water, and pour over your dandelion petals. Let this sit for half an hour to infuse.
3. Strain your concentrated tea mixture into a large pot, adding in the sugar, and your lemon juice. Bring this to a simmer, stirring and dissolving the sugar.
4. Once all the sugar is dissolved, add in your pectin, and continue cooking for a couple more minutes while stirring.
5. Pour your mixture into smaller sanitized jars, cover with lids, and set aside for the jelly to form.

WILD MINT

Mint is antimicrobial, and antispasmodic, and works great to relieve headaches and digestive disorders. It can also treat diarrhea, irritable bowel syndrome, and menstrual cramps, and improve respiratory complaints. It's a great homemade mouthwash and improves brain power/focus, waking you up well inhaled.

Harvest: Wild mint is common in wet areas, fields, and alongside small streams or creeks. You might notice that the plant blooms in the summer with beautiful purple/blue flowers. You only need to rub the leaves if you are unsure, and smell them. You can enjoy mint in all seasons that it grows, harvesting mostly the leaves.

Process: Dehydrate the leaves for tea mixtures, or keep them fresh in the fridge for mojitos, garnishing desserts, or to add to iced teas in the summer for a cool, refreshing taste.

Eat: Mint has a strong flavour. You can make a great jelly or pesto for lamb with it. I love it in my teas for digestion, boosting my focus and alertness. You can also slice it thinly (chiffonade) and use in your fruit salad.

SHEEP SORREL

This plant removes excess water from the body, helps with urinary and kidney complaints, as well as stress on your heart. Other helpful uses include reducing inflammation, diarrhea, excessive menstruation, and sore throats and mouth ulcers. A cousin of the dock family, it is considered to be a whole-body tonic, useful for detoxification and cell regeneration.

Harvest: Long, broad green leaves grow together. To harvest, use a pair of scissors to cut at the base. You will know it's sorrel by its beautiful lemony flavour and the jagged leaves starting at the base. It has a short stem before the leaf starts to widen.

Process: Back in the kitchen, remove the tough stems, leaving only the soft leaves. Soak the leaves in cold water and spin until dry. Store them in a sealed container for up to one week.

Eat: You can use this wild lettuce to make pestos or salad dressings. A great green to use in salad blends with its beautiful sourish lemon taste.

WILD ROSES

The hips contain high amounts of antioxidants and vitamins C, B3, D, and E, which are necessary for the body's general well-being. They are also antispasmodic, so they are used to treat asthma and other respiratory complications. The flowers moisturize the skin and bring a sense of love and peace to those who use them in their homes.

Harvest: In the summer, when the pink rose buds open into flowers. The pedals are very fragile and require a bag or basket that is breathable. Harvest only the flower petals instead of the whole bud if you want to have rose hips for fall. The hips are harvested in late fall after the first frost, and that is when they are the sweetest. Do not eat the little seeds inside the buds, as they contain small hairs that are harmful to the digestive system. Instead, you can eat them like an apple when in the field.

Process: Dry the hips and flower petals well in a dehydrator; they can mould if not dried thoroughly before storing. Be sure to use low heat when dehydrating the petals, as flower essence does not like high heat.

Eat: Infuse the flowers using very low heat for facial cleansing products (moisturizing) or simple syrups. You can dry the petals and add them to tea mixes for colour and beauty. I often decorate cakes or cupcakes with dried petals. Wild roses carry the energy of peace and happiness. They can also be used to wash one's home, bringing the whole family into a state of balance again. Energetically, roses are calming; traditionally, they are used to remove anger from the home. You can add the rose hips to teas, or stew them fresh (straining out the seeds), to make jelly spreads.

Notes: Pregnant women should <u>not use</u> wild rose; otherwise, it is a very safe herb to use topically or orally. Foraging for roses is an absolute joy; the soft petals are like silk to the fingertips. Be sure to dodge the thorny stems!

WILD HAZELNUTS

A great wild source of fat and fibre, hazelnuts also have many minerals and vitamins, such as magnesium, copper and manganese.

Harvest: Although the nut starts to form in the summer, hazelnuts are not harvestable until August. The end of summer can be a busy time for many of us, but you have to make time to harvest your hazelnuts before the squirrels get them all—I'm serious; timing the harvest is a real task. Collecting wild hazelnuts can be hard. You'll be quite a sight as you carry your ladder around the forest; you cannot climb the trees as they usually have long, thin branches. Hazelnut trees don't have one big trunk but rather many thin trunks, all coming from the same spot on the ground. The nuts grow solo, or sometimes in groups of 2, 3, or even 4. They will be encased in a cream-coloured shell that is, in turn, wrapped in a green leaf, shaped somewhat like a duck head with its beak. When the time is right for the nut to be harvested, the green leaf, which is the "beak," will start to open, and you will see the nutshell emerge.

Process: Dry your unshelled hazelnuts for a couple of days in a cool, dark place, allowing lots of air to flow between them all. Then peel off the leaves and crack each shell in half with a hammer or nut cracker to reveal the nut inside. This may be tedious, but it is way easier than shelling walnuts! Be grateful the hazelnut is there, in good condition.

Eat: You can enjoy hazelnuts raw or cooked. Roasting them at 350°F for 15 minutes brings out their flavour and caramelizes the sugars, giving them a delightful sweet nutty taste. Store them fully dried in a glass jar, and they will stay fresh for up to a month.

FORAGE & EAT WITH THE SEASONS

CHOCOLATE HAZELNUT SPREAD

What you'll need:

2 cups hazelnuts
½ cup melted chocolate
2 teaspoons vanilla extract
¼ cup ghee or oil

To Do:

1. Preheat the oven to 350°F. Place your shelled hazelnuts in a single layer on a shallow pan, then toast in the oven for 15-20 minutes, tossing them halfway through, until golden brown. Allow to cool fully.
2. Place the cooled nuts in a heavy-duty blender and blend well until they are small, little crumbs.
3. Add the melted chocolate, ghee and vanilla extract and blend at high speed until you have a smooth paste. Be sure to do this on high speed; I almost blew my Vitamix making this at low speed. It's a lot of work for your machine, but the taste is totally worth it.
4. Store in a clean jar and keep on the counter for 1 week, or refrigerate for 3 weeks (if you can hold off eating it that long). Use it as a spread, or make little chocolate truffles with it. If it gets hard or difficult to spread, blend in some nut milk and be sure to store it in the fridge.

LICORICE ROOT FERN

This plant is widely used to treat gastro problems, malaria, insomnia, and upper respiratory infections. It is 50 times sweeter than sugar and provides health benefits—a win-win. It also helps with heartburn, fatigue, eczema, and menopausal symptoms.

Harvest: Also known as sweet root, this fern usually grows within the moss on trees or rocks, hardly ever from the ground you walk on. You will find the fern leaves attached to one skinny stem that leads down to a thick root. It is easily identified and great for new foragers, especially kids.

Process: Harvest the root when in abundance, scraping off and discarding the outer bark once back in the kitchen. You can dry or use them fresh.

Eat: Its sweet root is a great choice for survival food, giving you natural sugars so that your brain can focus, filling your body with vigour and energy. Infuse the roots into vinegar for dressings. Add a dried root to your soups for some sweetness, or make a simple syrup from it when you reduce concentrated tea.

Cleavers

MEDICINAL HERBS

The plants in this section have been known for centuries, if not millennia, for their medicinal qualities. Some are eaten as food and/or dried to make teas. I make and serve wild herbal teas during most of my tours and workshops, and they are always a big hit. I often mix them with homegrown lemon balm or mint. You can also start to explore the realm of tincture-making and oil infusions using some of the herbs in this section. Being able to build your own home pharmacy is very empowering as a way to live more self-sufficiently and sustainably on this planet. Medicinal herbs can help with inflammation, wound healing, stretch marks, pain, and digestion.

ST. JOHN'S WORT

A St. John's wort tincture can be taken during the winter months for seasonal depression. Think of it this way: if the flowers capture pure sunlight (they sure look like it, with their beautiful yellow), and you store that in a jar, you can take some pure sunlight in the winter when you need it most. It is also a nervine, helping calm the nervous system. It can help reduce swelling and menstrual cramping. It has antiviral properties, is an antioxidant, and is antibacterial. This herb has a long stem, growing about 2 feet tall. The green leaves have a crisscross appearance because the leaf pairs attach at alternating angles. The flowers of St. John's Wort open towards the middle of summer, and they are bright yellow, just like the sun. When you pick the flowers and rub them with your fingers, they will leave a red or dark orange stain. Let the flowers dry slightly for a few hours, and then smash them to make oil infusions or alcohol tinctures. It's a fun herb to watch infuse, as it turns the oil red or the clear alcohol red in colour.

CLEAVERS

Also known as sticky weed, this plant is a great lymphatic supporter and mover. It helps move the waterways in the body, assisting with detoxification. It is a diuretic and can help relieve swollen lymph. It grows similar to a vine, sticking together as it crawls along the forest floor, or sometimes up tree trunks. The leaves on this plant make a star or a flower pattern, making it very appealing to the eye. In the summer, it will grow tiny little white flowers that will soon turn into seeds that can be roasted as a coffee substitute. I often gather this herb to take home and dry for tea. Or sometimes I will blanch it and chop it up, mixing it with my nettles into my spanakopitas. Eating my medicine up!

SELF-HEAL

Self-heal is a very gentle and very safe herb to work with. It is beneficial to the immune system, helps with gingivitis and wound healing, detoxifies the lymphatic system, and has antiviral properties. Around mid-summer, you may see a plant growing low to the ground with square stems, lanceolate to oval leaves, and green, hairy, spade-shaped bracts surrounding distinctive purple flowers. This herb is often found near homes, on lawns, and on forest trails. Be sure to harvest your herbs where there is no contamination from humans. Also called carpenter's herb, it is related to yarrow. Similar to yarrow, it is a styptic, meaning it stops bleeding when applied to a cut. Apply to cuts as a fresh herb, salve, or oil. Harvest it fresh for salads and cakes, or dry it for teas, salves, or tinctures. It is also anti-inflammatory when used inside the body for Crohn's, ulcers, and leaky gut syndrome. Use topically for cooling redness from rashes or eczema. Self-heal is a natural diuretic, so be cautious if you already take blood thinners. It is also used to help move toxins out of the body through the lymphatic system. In the laboratory, extracts of self-heal have been shown to disrupt the biofilm around certain viruses, thereby making it harder for the virus to enter cells.

MULLEIN

The leaves from Mullein are an expectorant, and it is often used to get rid of a deep, dry cough and many other respiratory disorders by helping the lungs rid themselves of mucus or tar. The flowers can be used topically to help with inflamed skin issues or as an ear oil. Mullein is hard to miss with its long, fuzzy green leaves that all grow from one center point, or baselet. In the first year it grows, its leaves stay low to the ground, and it does not flower. This is when I would harvest the leaves to dry for tea. Some people smoke it in little batches to help detox the lungs. In its second year of growth, it puts out its seeding and flowering head. Its yellow flowers resemble popcorn, as they bloom here and there in no particular order throughout the summer months. Collect the flowers to make a wonderful cough syrup for winter by infusing them into honey or sugar. Enjoy the process of working with flower essence, it is truly magical as you slowly collect the flowers throughout the days when they are ready to bloom.

YARROW

Yarrow, one of the oldest medicinal herbs, has been used since ancient times for healing wounds. It grows abundantly all around Canada on the sides of roads, fields, and forests—but there are many poisonous lookalikes, such as water hemlock, so you must know for sure, for sure, for sure that what you are harvesting is yarrow. The small white flowers of the yarrow plant grow in clusters atop long stems, and the leaves are fine and lacy. The leaves of the yarrow plant have anti-inflammatory and antioxidant properties; crush them up and apply topically to stop bleeding and keep wounds from getting infected. Yarrow tea is great for menstrual cramps. Collect what you need to make healing salves, teas, and first-aid bandages to have on hand. Harvest the flower clusters in early summer by cutting the stem just below them. Then harvest some leaves, but don't take them all—let some leaves remain on the plant so that it can bloom again!

GOLDENROD

Goldenrod is well known for its ability to treat urinary tract disorders and gastric upsets, as well as to aid the liver and the respiratory system. It can also be used topically to reduce pain and aid in the healing of burns, sores, skin irritation, and open wounds. Harvest only the green leaves and the yellow flowers from this plant; do not use the stem. Goldenrod grows tall, flowering mid to late summer; you will see its golden colour along the sides of roads, forests, and fields. If you have allergies in late summer, goldenrod is not to blame; it just gets confused with ragweed because they both have yellow flowers and they bloom around the same time. Ragweed is a wind pollinator; goldenrod is not. Infuse the fresh flowers into honey or add them to your baked goodies, such as muffins and cakes. Older flowers can be blended into powder to help thicken soups and stews as well.

RED CLOVER

This herb is anti-inflammatory, antispasmodic, and a diuretic. It is a safe herb for the whole family to use. It is taken to support brain health, reproductive health, and the lymphatic system, as well as for menopausal issues. It is also used topically for eczema, acne, rashes, athlete's foot, insect bites, and psoriasis. Red clover, also known as purple clover, appears in summer and has green stems and leaves and purple flowers. Dried, it can be used in teas or to decorate baked goods. It is also nicely infused into vinegar. Red clover is an excellent source of calcium, magnesium, phosphorus, potassium, and vitamins A and C. Cook it as a green leaf vegetable to add to any dish, or make a tincture.

SPRINGING INTO SUMMER

WILD HERBAL TEA

What you'll need:

Dried plantain leaf
Dried strawberry leaf
Dried dandelion leaf
Dried wild mint leaves
Dried mullein leaves
Dried red clover
Turkey tail mushroom, small chunks
Red-belted conk mushroom, small chunks

To Do:

1. Mix all the ingredients together. You can make enough for one cup of tea or make a larger batch and store it in a jar for later use. You can also add lemon balm and other medicinal herbs from your garden. Add dried berries for a fruity flavour or dried hibiscus that gives the tea a red colour while aiding the liver.

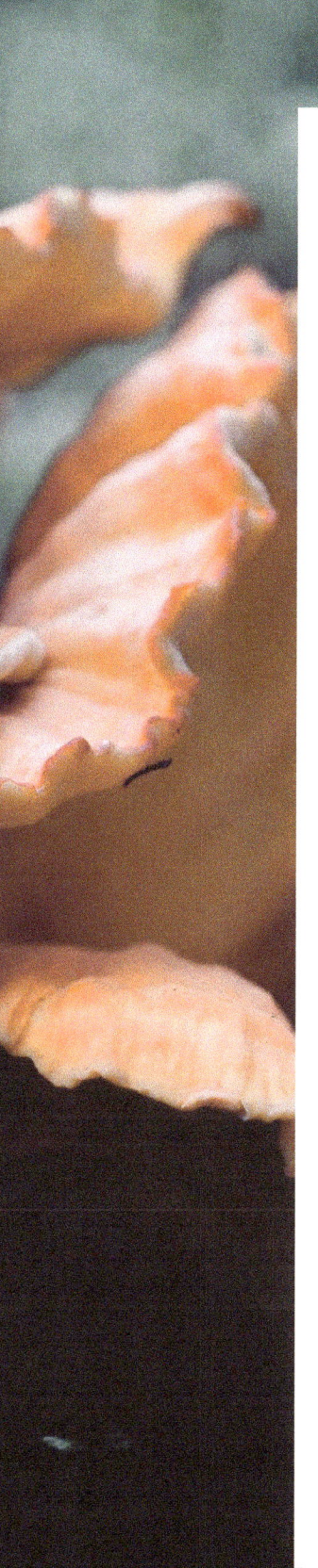

Fall

Welcome to the season of having fun with fungi. With the moistness of fall, we find thousands of mushroom varieties popping up from forest floors and decaying woods. During this time, you will find yourself downtown mushroom town (a forest or park that is full of mushrooms), experiencing the magic nature has to offer. Available in many different shapes and colors, this is the time of year when most of our edible varieties of mushrooms appear. If you find yourself overwhelmed, take a deep breath, and remember that nature will always give you what you need. Start yourself off by learning one new mushroom every year, finding new places to forage it, taking notes of when you harvested it, what type of forest you were in, and the elevation. The best of luck to you!

Let's start this cooler weather off with good footing and a strong immune system. Bone broth is already an amazing way to support the body during the fall and winter months. Homemade bone broth is better than store-bought. You can use the bones of any wild game, such as deer, grouse, moose, or even a mixture of bones, including beef and chicken. I save all my vegetable and herb trimmings in a ziplock bag in the freezer for when I'm ready to make broth instead of throwing them out. Bone broth is very beneficial to drink on its own, aiding the digestive system. It is a great first food after fasting, or when taking antibiotics.

MUSHROOM BONE BROTH

What you'll need:

2 ounces dried turkey tail mushroom
2 ounces dried red-belted conk mushroom
2 ounces dried artist conk mushroom
1 ounce dried chaga mushroom
1 ounce dried reishi mushroom
1 cup dried mushrooms, such as boletes
5 pounds Chicken or beef bones
2 onions, large, diced
3 carrots, diced, washed
6 celery sticks or vegetable and herb trimmings you have saved in the freezer
Cold water

To Do:

1. Roast the bones in the oven at 350°F until browned. Especially with red meat bones, roasting will give your broth a deeper, richer flavour and a darker colour.
2. Place bones in a large pot, followed by your vegetable scraps, mushrooms and herbs.
3. Fill the pot with cold water (starting with cold water extracts more nutrients from the dense bone.)
4. Place on high heat just long enough to bring your mixture up to a simmer, then reduce heat and simmer low and slow for 6 to 8 hours (or overnight for red meat bones). Simmering your bone broth is key; boiling will make it cloudy.
5. Strain out the solids, and you are ready to enjoy your broth as is or make it into a soup. Season with soy sauce, worcestershire, and a little spice if you are enjoying it on its own.

RED-BELTED CONK

This mushroom has an orange and/or red ring around the edge of it. Sometimes it is quite dark on top, and only a small orange line can be seen with the white line. Related to the reishi, the red-belted conk can look similar, but it is much tougher and harder. Red-belted conks are found abundantly in younger forests. Over time, it grows from the size of a thumbnail to the size of a dinner plate! Make sure the underside is white before harvesting. Harvest only the outer edge of this fungus so it can stay in the forest and continue to grow. The edges and underlining gills have the most medicinal properties anyway, so there's really no need to bring the whole thing home to process. This mushroom is very abundant in British Columbia and is often overlooked as useless. Little do we know, it's waiting to help us. When blended into powder, this mushroom can be used in your first aid kit for cuts. It coagulates the blood to stop bleeding, and it helps prevent infection at the same time with its antibacterial and anti-microbial properties.

TURKEY TAIL

Turkey tail boosts your immune system, has antioxidants, and heals the gut by balancing its bacteria. It is smaller in size, thin like leather, and the colours are layered just like a turkey's tail, with grays and browns. This mushroom is used in China to fight cancer, where their medical system accepts it. Turkey tail grows in clusters on old lumber and rotting trees. I have used turkey tail mushrooms for my dog's allergies, along with other natural remedies suggested by naturopathic veterinarians. I infuse this mushroom regularly in my teapot. Beware of its lookalike, the rusty-gilled polypore, which has orange stripes and is not useful. Be sure the gills are white when harvesting, if not, it has started to go bad already.

ARTIST CONK

Artist conk supports the respiratory systems, and immune systems, and is readily used during cold and flu season. This shelf mushroom has a chocolate brown colour on top and white underneath. When you touch or scratch the white gills, they bruise to a dark brown colour! Therefore you can draw on them, which is a super fun activity for kids to do before taking the conks home to dry for medicine. This is the only shelf mushroom whose gills bruise in this way, so you know you have an artist's conk when it does. You can use this mushroom to make your own mushroom hot chocolate! Simply dry, and blend into powder and mix with cocoa.

Here, you can see our Plantwave music machine hooked up to an artist's conk. It reads the mushroom's vibrational frequency and turns it into music for us to listen to. We offer workshops so that others may experience Plantwave music.

Medicinal mushrooms

REISHI

Reishi mushroom has been used to help enhance the immune system, reduce stress, improve sleep, and lessen fatigue. People also take reishi mushrooms for health conditions such as high blood pressure and high cholesterol. This mushroom can be hard to find as it grows only in the oldest of forests, where loggers have not logged as much. It is the most popular and most medicinal mushroom of them all. It is the softest of the shelf mushrooms, sometimes cooked and eaten in a soup. Its colour ranges from orangey brown to bright orange, and its surface is often shiny. It has a little stem-like structure with white gills. The size of this mushroom varies widely, from as small as a small hand to as big as a 2-person table!

MEDICINAL MUSHROOMS

Harvest conk or shelf mushroom species when they have white gills underneath; this ensures they are in a prime state full of medicinal properties. We extract the medicinal properties from these mushrooms by soaking them in water or alcohol. I often add them to my teapot for a week or so, infusing their medicine into the water every time it boils for tea, coffee, or hot chocolate for the whole family to get its benefits. You can also make alcohol tinctures from conks. Sometimes, we infuse the mushrooms first in water and then in alcohol to extract the different chemical compounds. Making medicinal mushroom tinctures are most helpful when you use multiple species together, for example, turkey tail and red-belted conk.

* Chanterelles

CHANTERELLES

Full of zinc, antioxidants, copper, and vitamin D, chanterelle mushrooms are a great addition to any culinary delight you might wish to cook up.

Harvest: Golden chanterelles literally look like gold hiding in the moss. Sometimes only a small corner of the golden mushroom will appear. Therefore, walking slowly in the forest is always the way to forage. Since the mycelium network for this mushroom species is underground, all varieties of chanterelles grow on the ground rather than on dead trees. You will find them in small groups, or in large groups, which we call patches. Note the locations of these patches with your GPS when you find them so you can return to them year after year. Cut this mushroom at the base of the stem with a knife so you don't put extra dirt in your bags (making more work for you when you get home). The gills of chanterelles are lined and extend down the stem. They are a light cream-yellow colour versus the dark yellower cap. There are also white, blue, black, and pink chanterelles, all looking a little different. The winter chanterelle, also known as the funnel chanterelle or yellowfoot, is literally shaped like a funnel, with a hole going down from the middle of the cap into the stem, making the stem hollow. Winter chanterelles appear from October into December and can withstand some frost making them a winter mushroom. They grow in abundance.

Process: Using a soft brush, dust off any forest debris before bringing chanterelles home to your kitchen. The golden chanterelle peels apart easily like string cheese, revealing white flesh inside, making knife work unnecessary. They smell like apricots in some cases. Winter changes can have little dark dots on the gills, soak and wash them for the best results. If you have foraged in the rain, your mushrooms may be soggy, simply lay out a towel and keep them out on your counter for the night. Package and store them in brown bags or open baskets so they can breathe in your fridge for up to two weeks.

Eat: You can sauté all types of chanterelles to go with egg dishes, pasta sauces (creamy or red), or stir-fries. The best way to preserve chanterelles is by sautéing and freezing them in small, portioned bags. You can dry them, but the texture may be tough afterward. We usually enjoy them fresh, cooking with them daily!

CHANTERELLE ANTIPASTO

What you'll need:

1 litre vegetable oil
1 litre white vinegar
4 cups chanterelles
6 carrots, peeled
6 ribs celery
3 cups fresh green and yellow beans
1 head cauliflower
3 bell peppers, mixed colours
3 cups fresh pearl onions
2 jars stuffed green olives, drained
2 cans sliced black olives, drained
1 small can tomato paste
1 jar forest capers or regular capers
4 cans tuna, drained (you could also use local salmon or trout)
1 tablespoon sea salt
1 tablespoon ground black pepper
1 tablespoon red chilli flakes

To Do:

1. In a large pot, bring the oil and vinegar to a simmer. Small-dice the mushrooms, carrots, celery, beans, and cauliflower, then add them to the pot. Simmer for one minute, stirring occasionally.
2. Dice the peppers and add them to the pot along with the pearl onions. Simmer for another 5 minutes. Then add the rest of the ingredients and continue to stew on low heat for 10 minutes.
3. Store in sterilized jars in the refrigerator for up to one month, or pressure can for your pantry shelf.

MUSHROOM SLOPPY JOES

What you'll need:

1 onion, diced small
1 pound chanterelles, chopped
Butter for sautéing
1 pound ground beef or venison
1/2 cup ketchup
¼ cup mustard
¼ cup relish
4 to 6 buns
4 to 6 slices of your favourite cheese (optional)

To Do:

1. Sauté the diced onion in butter until lightly caramelized, then add your chopped mushrooms and sauté until everything is lightly browned.
2. Add the ground meat, cooking for 5 minutes, then add the ketchup, mustard, and relish, cooking for 8 minutes on low.
3. Now you have the option to melt cheese on top of your meat sauce, or on the buns. Ladle this meaty mushroom sauce onto buns and enjoy.

SHAGY MANES

The nutrient profile for these mushrooms is vitamin B, potassium, and phosphorus, and have been known to help fight cancer. They have antioxidants, are anti-inflammatory, and can help with brain function.

Harvest: Shaggy manes are a beginner-friendly mushroom that is widely known and delicious. It can be found in fields, paddocks, roadsides, and even lawns. (Mushrooms absorb what is in their environment, so if you are harvesting them from a lawn, be sure they have not been sprayed with chemicals.) Shaggy manes grow quickly, taking only about 2 to 3 days to mature. When young, these mushrooms have a white stem, white gills, and a white and brown cap with little hairs that look like a shaggy haircut. As the mushroom matures, the gills turn from white to pink to brown and finally black. You will not see the gills until the mushroom is older and starts to open up, therefore, slice it in half when picking the young ones to help confirm your identification.

Process: Because this mushroom often bursts out of dirt or gravel, you will need to dust or gently wipe off the dirt from the cap. Slice them in half right away and dehydrate. Shaggy manes will not last in your fridge for days on end like other mushrooms; they will continue to age until they turn into black ink, which you can then use for art projects!

Eat: Cook shaggy manes the day you harvest or the day after—before they ink up. Chop them into small pieces and sauté in butter or olive oil. This mushroom is versatile, similar to white button mushrooms you buy in the grocery store, giving any dish you make with them a savoury, umami flavour.

Pear-shaped Puffballs

PUFFBALLS

Puffballs contain a great amount of potassium, and are a good source of protein. They promote homeostasis and muscle regeneration, are prized medicinally in China, and are anti-inflammatory.

Harvest: Many varieties of puffballs are edible, and they grow in a range of environments. In a mossy forest, you will find the dusky puffball or the white gem-studded puffball singly or in clusters. Along roadsides or fields, you will find the pear-shaped puffball, white and light brown on the top, which usually grows in clusters. In fields and grasslands, you can find giant white puffballs the size of your dinner plate! Slice all your puffballs in half to ensure they are pure white and solid inside; anyone with discolouration has gone bad and should not be used. Puff balls are the famous mushrooms you find in fields after they have gone bad, that puff out brown smoke (its spores). Kids often like to play with them and almost everyone has come across them at least once.

Process: They are great dehydrated, but we often just eat them fresh. No cleaning is required unless they are picked in gravel, then you should wash them

Eat: Sauté with bacon fat if you swing that way, and enjoy on top of a steak. Small puffballs cooked whole will give your dish a very unique appearance. Puffballs are great on pizza, as are all the fall mushrooms in this book.

HEDGEHOGS

This mushroom can help strengthen your bones, help nerve functions, fight off viruses, and increase sex hormones. It is a great source of protein, calcium, vitamins D & C, iron, and potassium. They are anti-inflammatory and antibacterial.

Harvest: I have found hedgehog mushrooms as low as sea level and as high as 2000 metres above sea level. They can be small or large. They have thick stems, and they always grow from the ground. Yellow or golden in colour, they resemble chanterelles at first, but once you pick them, you will see that the gills are small and pointy like their namesake animal, the hedgehog. The gills break off when agitated or brushed, so it's a good idea to place them carefully in baskets after harvesting, being sure not to move them around much.

Process: Gently brush off any forest debris when you get home. You can slice and dehydrate them, then store them in a glass jar for up to a year. Or you can slice and sauté them, portion them into small ziplock bags, and store them in the freezer. Store in your refrigerator for up to two weeks in a brown paper bag or basket so they can breathe.

Eat: My favourite dish to make with hedgehog mushrooms is chicken and mushroom cream sauce with pasta. Sauté the mushrooms first to caramelize the sugars; you will surely enjoy this dish. The texture is similar to that of chanterelles, so you can use this mushroom in any of the chanterelle recipes.

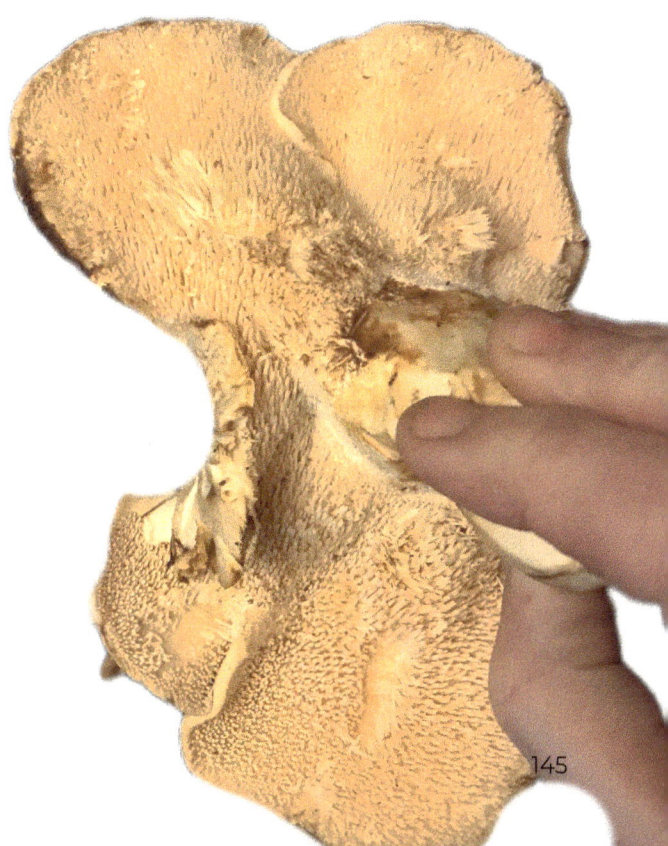

FORAGE & EAT WITH THE SEASONS

CREAMY HEDGEHOG MUSHROOM SAUCE

What you'll need:

1 large onion, medium dice
2 carrots, peeled and chopped
4 ribs celery, chopped
1 pound hedgehog mushrooms, chopped
3 cloves garlic, diced
100g flour
250 ml chicken stock or vegetable stock
2 bay leaves
10g fresh thyme and other fresh herbs
250ml heavy cream
Salt, pepper, and cayenne pepper to taste

To Do:

1. In a large pot, sauté the diced onion in your choice of fat until lightly browned.
2. Add the chopped carrots, celery, and mushrooms, and sauté until things start to look cooked and caramelized. Then add the garlic and cook lightly.
3. Sprinkle in the flour, then stir and cook for about 3 to 4 minutes. Start adding the stock slowly, stirring constantly, so there are no lumps. When it starts to thicken, add the rest of the stock and stir.
4. Add 2 bay leaves and simmer on low for 30 minutes.
5. Add the heavy cream, thyme, salt, pepper, and cayenne pepper. Make sure not to boil after the cream is added, or it will separate.
6. Enjoy this mushroom sauce with your favourite pasta, or dip sourdough bread into it. Alternatively, you can add more broth to make this more of a soup, which is great on a rainy fall day with homemade dumplings.

MUSHROOM POWDER SEASONING

What you'll need:

Dried chanterelles, boletes, morels, or any other culinary mushroom

To Do:

1. Dry mushrooms until they are crispy—mix different varieties of mushrooms for a range of flavours.
2. Pulverize the dried mushrooms with a blender or a mortar and pestle. Store the powder in an airtight container.
3. Use your mushroom powder to season whole chicken or beef roasts before you roast them or to flavour gravies and sauces.

FALL

BEAR'S TOOTH MUSHROOM

Closely related to the lion's mane, bear's tooth is an antidepressant and antioxidant that helps with anxiety, brain function, and memory retention. It is a great source of fibre, thiamine, riboflavin, manganese, zinc, and potassium.

Harvest: Always found on dead trees or logs in mixed wood forests, this big, white mushroom can be spotted from 75 yards away! It is honestly magnificent. Bear's tooth has a white coral-like mass with white gills that hang down like icicles. It has a white spore print and a beautifully sweet smell. Make sure it is nice and white, and not starting to rot. Some discolouration is okay; it just means it's getting older. Discard if it has mold.

Process: Because of this mushroom's coral-like texture, it has many nooks and crannies for debris to get into. Dry out this mushroom whole on your countertop overnight if picked during rainy days, and then tip it upside down and tap it with your hand to get most of the debris out. If needed, you can then give it a little soak in a bowl of water with some salt to get rid of any bugs. Sauté and freeze in small bags for easy cooking later on, versus dehydrating.

Eat: Bear's tooth mushrooms are kind of like chicken, white, meaty, and juicy. Sautéing will remove any extra moisture, which can be helpful if you harvest them after a rain. We love bear's tooth in our fried rice instead of meat. It also works great for tacos, mushroom jerky, chunky mushroom and vegetable cream soups, and of course stir-fry.

149

Bear's Tooth Mushroom

MUSHROOM JERKY

What you'll need:

1 to 2 pounds bear's tooth mushrooms
1 tablespoon soy sauce
1 tablespoon hoisin sauce
½ teaspoon dried or fresh chili peppers
¼ teaspoon powdered ginger
¼ teaspoon garlic powder

To Do:

1. Cut up your bear's tooth mushrooms into long pieces that won't fall through the racks of your dehydrator.
2. Sauté the pieces in a dry pan until they start to caramelize. Then add in the sauces, chillies, and spices. Cook for 4 minutes, then turn off the burner and let the mushroom pieces cool in the pan. As they cool, they will absorb flavour.
3. Line your dehydrator racks with silicone mats or parchment paper so little pieces of mushroom won't fall through and make a mess. Spread your mushrooms out evenly and dehydrate on low heat for about 6 hours or until your mushroom jerky reaches the desired consistency (chewy).

CHICKEN OF THE WOODS

This mushroom is very high in minerals and vitamins; mothers have used it after childbirth to support recovery. It is full of antioxidants and is used as an anti-inflammatory.

Harvest: Chicken of the woods is found on dead and decaying trees, often big Douglas firs. It is bright orange and yellow on top, has yellow pored gills, and has white flesh inside. It is a shelf mushroom, and when abundant, it sometimes resembles a ladder for fairies and gnomes to climb. It can grow on the sides of trees and under them. Make sure your specimen is fresh and spongy, with vibrant colours and no sign of molds. Do not harvest the older, dry ones, as they can be tough and may make you sick. Be careful when consuming alcohol with this mushroom, as some people have an adverse reaction to the combination. Before eating, make sure the underside is still a clean yellow.

Process: Chicken of the woods tears nicely by hand, like chanterelles. Sauté and freeze in portions. You can also bread chunks with flour, eggs, and bread crumbs, then freeze them for easy meals later down the road. Dehydrating is also an option, but it can give the mushroom a tough texture when you go to reconstitute it. Consuming fresh is best, only taking from the forest what you need.

Eat: I like to grab a couple of breaded pieces from the freezer, fry them up nice and crispy, and add them to a zesty Caesar salad. Chicken of the woods also goes great with tomato sauces; my recipe for "chicken" parmesan sandwiches is below. Pan-frying the breaded pieces on their own until crispy is always great, as they turn out just like chicken strips! You can barely tell that it is a mushroom when you dip it into a chipotle or lime aioli.

CHICKEN OF THE WOODS NUGGETS

What you'll need:

Chicken of the woods or bear's tooth mushrooms
2 eggs
Flour
Breadcrumbs
Seasonings, as desired

To Do:

1. Cut your mushrooms into large strips or chunks.
2. Whisk the eggs in a bowl. Put the flour in another bowl, and put your breadcrumbs in a separate bowl as well.
3. Place your mushrooms in the flour first for a light dusting, then over to the egg wash, then over to your breadcrumbs.
4. Freeze on a tray, or fry right away in a good amount of oil in a hot pan and enjoy right away with a variety of dipping sauces.

CHICKEN OF THE WOODS PARMESAN SANDWICHES

What you'll need:

Chicken of the woods mushrooms
Butter for sautéing
1 white onion sliced
Tomato sauce
Sandwich buns
Parmesan

To Do:

1. Shred the mushrooms using your hands.
2. Melt butter in a pan. Sauté the onions until they get some colour, then add your shredded mushrooms. Allow the mushrooms to cook and release their moisture, then lightly caramelize them for about 6 minutes.
3. Reduce the heat, add the tomato sauce, and simmer very low for 8 minutes. Do not boil your tomato sauce, as it can get bitter.
4. Open up your sandwich buns and arrange them on a sheet pan. Add your mushroom mixture, and top with lots of Parmesan. Bake at 400°F for 10-15 minutes, until the cheese is melted and golden brown.

ADMIRABLE BOLETE (VELVET BOLETE)

It helps to regulate blood pressure and heart problems with its low sodium and high potassium content. Rich in fibre and antioxidants, it helps with inflammation. As are most wild mushrooms, the Admiral bolete is also high in zinc, iron, copper, manganese, and B-vitamins.

Harvest: This mushroom grows from the ground and is found only in the fall. With its beautiful purple stem and velvety purple cap, the admirable bolete is part of the polypore family, with yellow pores on the underside that get darker with age. When the weather is right (rainfalls alternating with sun), young, admirable boletes can be found all fall. Their dark caps make them a little tricky to spot, but once your eyes get used to what you are looking for, you will find more and more. The cap is fuzzy like velvet, and gets light spots as it ages. If you find larger specimens, slice them in half to check for bugs before removing them from the forest. This way, you can leave the spores and any parts of the mushroom that you don't want in the forest where they belong to decay, and support the ecosystem.

Process: Slice and dehydrate; this will give your mushrooms more texture and flavour as they can be slimy when cooked fresh. As they age in a jar, add bay leaves or other dry herbs. Fresh, admirable boletes will last a week in your refrigerator. Keep them uncovered so they can breathe oxygen like all your mushrooms

Eat: Whether fresh or dehydrated, this mushroom has a nice lemony flavour. Dehydrate and blend into fine powder, then use it to coat your chicken wings or a whole chicken. It will enhance the umami flavour of any meat while adding minerals and vitamins to your dish. Sauté it fresh for a stir-fry or pasta dish too!

FALL

KING BOLETE (PORCINI)

Rich in carbohydrates, fibre, and proteins, this mushroom is also full of B-vitamins. It is also a good source of minerals such as manganese, zinc, and selenium. However, these minerals will degrade when the mushroom gets older or is stored in the fridge for too long.

Harvest: In late summer to fall, as this is when you will find the largest of all the boletes growing: the King Bolete. At the head of the class in terms of flavour and texture, this is your prized bolete. The cap is usually brown or, in some cases, tan. The thick stem is what gives it away to be a king. Before harvesting, tap the cap of the mushroom to release any extra spores onto the forest floor. This will ensure you have more mushrooms to return to next year! Yes, King Boletes and other mushrooms will grow year after year in the same location. This is why mushroom pickers hardly ever share their spots with others. You can either cut or pull this mushroom, but if you pull it, be sure to clean it off before storing it in your bag so you don't make a mess of it. If it is larger and older, be sure to check for worms by slicing the stem and cap in half. If it is wormy, leave it in the forest so it can decay and nourish future mushrooms.

Process: Enjoy fresh from your refrigerator for up to a week and a half. After that, slice and dehydrate them. Dehydrating changes and enhances the flavour as well as the texture. It makes a great mushroom powder for seasoning meats and gravies or as holiday gifts.

Eat: Slice and bread king bolete like you would a pork cutlet. Fry until crispy on both sides, then enjoy with an aioli or on top of a Caesar salad. It also goes great in soups, stews, and sauces.

SECOND-CLASS BOLETE VARIETIES

Harvest: The second-class bolete varieties are not as amazing in flavor or texture, but you can still enjoy them in your home. All growing in the fall, Boletes are a large family of mushrooms, all with pores rather than gills. Most have skinny stems, such as Zeller's bolete (pinkish-purple stem and a dark brown cap) and the western-painted suillus (brown and yellow fuzzy cap with yellow gills). If it stains blue when cut, it is a blue-staining Jack; these are not highly regarded. The short stemmed slippery Jack is edible when you peel off the top layer of the cap, not ideal, but still edible, hence these are second class mushrooms, not gourmet mushrooms.

Process: These varieties of boletes can be slimy when cooked and not very flavorful. Slice them, then dehydrate to improve the texture. For more flavour, add a bay leaf to the jar you store them in. Europeans love to do this, and they value their mushrooms very highly, adding them to Christmas soups and for special occasions.

Eat: Simply soak your dried mushrooms for 5 minutes before cooking with them. If you're making a soup, you can add them to the soup and then simmer. You can also grind your dried mushrooms into fine powder and use the powder to flavour stews, sauces, and gravies. Some people (myself included) don't like slimy mushrooms, so powdering them is a delightful way to get their minerals, nutrients, and flavours into a dish. I will add these dried second class boletes to bone broths or stocks for extra flavour and nutrients.

PINE MUSHROOM OR MATSUTAKE

Supportive to the immune system, anti-inflammatory, and loaded with antioxidants, this mushroom can help protect the liver and combat diabetes and tumors. This mushroom is full of vitamins and minerals.

Harvest: This mushroom is found in pine, spruce, hemlock, or douglas fir forests in the fall. The pine mushroom has a white or slightly yellowish cap, and the gills are white when fresh and turn a cinnamon colour with age. If it is a "button" (young), the veil will cover the gills and form a ring around the stem. What is unique about the pine mushroom is the smell, often described as spicy, cinnamony, pungent, earthy, or sweet. Squirrels love to eat this mushroom and will often dig them up during the fall months, leaving you with a helpful clue as to the location of a patch. To hunt pine mushrooms yourself, you will first need to find a "flag"—an older one that has opened up. Then you can start to look down at your feet for the tops of little ones just beginning to emerge from the ground. Get down on your hands and knees and dig them up, then fill the holes back in to cover and protect the mycelium underneath. This also helps to keep your find a secret from other mushroom pickers. After the 1970s and '80s, when their supplies started to dwindle, we started to ship this beautiful mushroom overseas to Japan. Their culture readily values this mushroom. My hope is that you and I can enjoy this beautiful mushroom as well.

Process: Use a soft brush to remove any forest debris, then moderately trim off the dirt at the bottom of the stem. Slice and dry for winter months, or enjoy them fresh. Fresh ones will last a long time in your fridge.

Eat: Slice thick, then dredge in flour, egg, and bread crumbs and fry on high heat to get a crispy cutlet. Enjoy with your favourite dipping sauce. Roasting in the oven also works great, as does steaming with rice.

PICKLED MUSHROOMS

NOTE: As always, be sure you know for sure, for sure, for sure, what mushrooms or wild food products you have harvested. Many mushroom articles online will say you cannot pickle wild mushrooms. This is due to past incidents in which people pickled a poisonous species.

What you'll need:

2 pounds fresh, young, firm mushrooms
2 cloves garlic
½ cup oil
1 teaspoon salt
¾ cup water
½ cup white wine vinegar or rice wine vinegar
4 sprigs thyme
1 bay leaf

To Do:

1. Clean up your young mushrooms by trimming away older or damaged bits and rinsing with cold water. Lay them out on a clean kitchen towel to dry.
2. Thinly slice your garlic and sauté in the oil in a large pot on medium heat. Do not burn the garlic; watch it and stir it constantly.
3. Once the garlic has become golden brown, add in your mushrooms and sauté until all its juices have been released and the mushrooms are starting to brown lightly.
4. Add the water and vinegar, and bring it all to a simmer for 5 minutes.
5. Fill a sanitized glass jar with your pickled mushrooms, adding the fresh herbs. Stir the mixture so any bubbles can come to the top; air bubbles contain oxygen that will make the mushrooms go bad. Be sure to weigh down the mushrooms so they are entirely below the oil layer. The oil will keep them from going bad. Preservation at its finest.
6. Store in the fridge for up to one month, or pressure-can to preserve on the shelf.

LOBSTER MUSHROOM

Harvest: The Lobster mushroom is technically not a mushroom but a parasitic fungus that grows on certain species of Russula and Lactarius mushrooms, turning them a bright orange or red colour. It is found on the ground of coniferous and deciduous forests in late summer to early fall. Its bright colour is easily spotted if not fully covered by moss and debris. You will know it is a lobster mushroom because it will smell exactly like seafood. Lobster mushrooms give off a white spore print, so there may be white "dust" present when you come across this firm, dense mushroom. When harvesting, be sure to check them for worms so you can leave any discards in the forest to support future growth. Dust off as much of the forest as you can before placing the mushrooms in your basket or bag.

Process: Slice and dehydrate for a powder, or sauté, then portion into small ziplock bags, and freeze.

Eat: Lobster mushrooms have a dense texture similar to that of meat. Enjoy them in a beautiful seafood risotto, or add them to your next seafood chowder recipe. They are also great on their own, sliced and fried on each side until caramelized well.

LOBSTER MUSHROOM CHOWDER

What you'll need:

1 large onion, diced small
2 carrots, peeled and diced small
3 ribs celery, diced small
2 lobster mushrooms
¾ cup butter
3 cloves garlic
¾ cup flour
1 litre seafood stock or chicken
2 cups corn
1 bay leaf
2 tablespoons fresh thyme leaves
1 cup diced halibut, cod, and or prawns
1 cup heavy cream

To Do:

1. In a large pot with your fat of choice, sauté the diced onion, carrots, and celery until the onion is translucent. Then add your diced mushrooms and sauté until caramelized.
2. Add butter and garlic, then cook for 1 minute just to get the flavours of the garlic going. Then, reduce the heat and stir in the flour.
3. Add stock 1 cup at a time, whisking well each time so there are no lumps.
4. Add corn, bay leaf, and thyme. Bring the soup to a boil while stirring continuously. Then, reduce the heat to low and simmer lightly for 10 minutes.
5. Add your seafood of choice, simmer for 5 more minutes, then finish by stirring in the heavy cream. Do not boil after this point.

Truffle fungi

Winter

Winter is that time of the year when you start to cook with more of your wild preserved foods. There really isn't much to harvest during this season. This may be a good time to process and strain the oils and tinctures you've been neglecting. Indulge in your foraged abundance: open some long-awaited pickled wild asparagus, or pickles from the garden, dried mushrooms, and infused salts. Sprinkle your baths with dried wild rose petals and lavender, and enjoy time spent inside, keeping cozy with apple ciders. If the winter is mild, there may still be winter chanterelles to harvest for a special winter Solstice celebration.

A nice way to keep enjoying fresh greens in the winter is to grow your own microgreens or sprouts. Alfalfa sprouts on the countertop are super easy, just rinse twice a day, and they are ready within 6 days. This way, you have fewer trips to the grocery store, and you get fresh, crisp greens grown with your own water, love and intentions.

You can also prepare to tap different species of trees for their deliciously sweet sap. Birch trees, maple trees, and walnut trees are some of the most commonly tapped trees in Canada and BC. It is just so gratifying to be able to harvest your own sugars, electrolytes, and minerals.

FORAGE & EAT WITH THE SEASONS

BIG LEAF MAPLES

This tree often has licorice fern growing within the moss. These mini organisms are called epiphytes. This tree's flowers, also called wild broccoli, are edible in spring. Maple water is harvestable after the Winter Solstice when temperatures are freezing during the night and above 0 during the day. It takes 60 to 70 litres of maple water to make 1 litre of maple syrup. Maple trees rely on the freeze-and-thaw cycle of the weather to get their waters flowing through the cambium layer (inner bark) of the tree. When harvesting maple water, start by sanitizing all your equipment and drilling a small hole into the trunk of the tree, about 4 feet up. Then insert your spiles with a hose that goes down to your bucket and is attached to the side of your bucket for collection. Drinking maple water alone is super beneficial for the throat and helps to rebuild muscles after a big workout. Some people freeze their maple water and then defrost it all together to boil it down into one big maple syrup pot. You will need all day to make syrup, simmering it outside for all the water to evaporate. I personally tend to drink the sweet tree water fresh or heat it up in my teapot, using the tree water instead of tap water to make my coffee or tea. When consumed fresh, the water is loaded with electrolytes and minerals such as calcium, zinc and magnesium.

WINTER

OTHER TREES TO TAP

On the East Coast of Canada, the most common and number one choice of maple tree tapping is the Sugar maple, followed by the Black maple, Red maple, Silver maple, and lastly, the Norway maple. Identify your tree species in the summer or fall so you can use the leaves as a primary indicator.

Secondary trees to tap include the paper birch and yellow birch. Paper birch has the highest sugar content. Yellow birch has the highest amount of antioxidants, and the sugar content is lower than that of the maple birch (acer species). You can also tap alder trees, which have a spicy flavour, or nut trees. I have gathered sap from butternut walnut trees in BC. It is deliciously sweet, and when reduced down by cooking, a clearer gelatinous syrup is made vs the amber colour that appears when making maple syrup.

171

MAPLE SYRUP

What you'll need:

60 litres tree sap (or whatever amount you have on hand)
1 large pot
1 outdoor cooking stove

To Do:

1. Reserve about 4 hours in your day to observe and frequently stir your boiling pot of maple water. It is best to do this outdoors as the process will release a lot of steam.
   Get a large pot, the largest you can find, add the sap and begin boiling, stirring every now and then.
2. Pay close attention when you get down to the last couple of inches of darker water in the pot. I won't lie, there have been times I neglected to watch it, and the sugar all burnt to a crisp!
3. Once the water level is reduced, transfer the amber-coloured water into a small pot and bring it inside to finish on the stove. Water boils at 212°F, so boil and stir until your mixture reaches 216°F-218°F. At that point, all the water is gone, leaving you with only the sugar!

SEAWEEDS AND SHELLFISH

Sea vegetables have copious amounts of proteins, vitamins, iodine and calcium that are readily available and abundant. Best harvested in winter in clean oceans (away from large cities), seaweed also helps the body get rid of toxins - sodium alginate from the seaweed bonds with toxins and heavy metals, and flushes them out of the system. Spas often offer seaweed wraps, where they wrap the whole body in seaweed for a period, allowing the body to suck in the nutrients through your skin, your largest organ. This is called thalassotherapy, using our largest organ, the skin.

Sustainable harvesting practices are very important in this type of foraging. The presence of seaweed, kelps, sea beans, and other greens is very important for our oceans' ecosystems. Therefore, beach harvesting is the most sustainable practice of ocean vegetable foraging. Seaweeds and kelps will attach themselves with an anchor to a rock at the bottom of the ocean to keep them in their tidal zone. Cut the seaweed from the anchor so it can continue to grow.

Sea asparagus is by far one of our favourites: its crunchy and perfectly salty flesh goes well with scrambled eggs or stir fry. It can also be pickled. There are also bull kelp norris, sea beans, and sea lettuce that can be harvested from the ocean.

January and February are the dominant months for harvesting vegetables and shellfish from the ocean. Harmful bacteria, such as red tide, are not able to flourish during this colder time.

As for shellfish, you can get everything you see in the restaurants in the wild. Mussels, gooey ducks, oysters, clams, and crustaceans such as crabs are all up for harvesting as long as you follow the local fishing and harvesting regulations. This means not harvesting on shellfish farms, and having a valid saltwater license for crabbing and prawning. Local BC spot prawns are delicious, I think we should be eating them more regularly versus shipping them overseas. A lot of the shellfish we buy from the grocery stores in North America are actually shipped from overseas – Thailand, Indonesia, etc. The list goes on of inhumane fishing practices done to the earth and people so we in America can have cheap prawns and seafood. Unfortunately, the industry is quite corrupt. So it is up to us, the consumers, to choose to eat local and vote with our dollar.

WINTER BAKING PROJECTS

With the extra downtime in winter, working with sourdough is a great way to enhance your home food culture. Sourdough not only adds a nice tangy flavour to your bread or pancakes, it also promotes the health of your digestive system as the natural yeast culture starts to break down the flour proteins before they even reach your stomach. Creating your own sourdough starter is simple; it just takes some attention and time, but the reward is beautiful.

SOURDOUGH STARTER RECIPE

What you'll need:

Flour
Filtered water (not chlorinated city water)
Love

To Do:

Day 1: Mix 100g of flour and 100g of water in a glass mason jar with a wooden spoon. As you stir, add in your intentions of health and gratitude. Cover with a breathable top and store in a warm place. Name your starter.

Day 2: Discard half of your mixture from the glass jar and add another 100g of flour and 100g of water. Mix with a wooden spoon.

Day 3: Repeat steps from day 2, discarding half and feeding your starter. Do this for 6 days, and on the seventh day, you will have a strong sourdough starter that you can use in recipes. When you're not using your sourdough starter, if you're going away or you just don't have time to do sourdough every day, you can place your starter in the fridge to reduce the yeast activity, slowing it down from eating the fresh flour. Be sure to "feed" it before retiring it to the fridge.

Notes: You can use the discarded content in many ways; my quickest and simplest is to make a pancake. Add salt and pepper, cayenne, dried nettle, and green onions to the pancake to make it savoury. Or if you would like to make it sweet, just add some blueberries while cooking, and enjoy with maple syrup.

SOURDOUGH BREAD RECIPE

Notes: We will be making 2 doughs, one with the sourdough starter and the other without, then we will combine the 2 at the end.

DOUGH 1 (LEVAIN DOUGH)

150g bakers blend flour or all-purpose flour
150g filtered warm water
12g mature starter (this is the active starter you fed hours before.)

To Do:

1. Mix everything together with a wooden spoon and cover it with a damp cloth that does not touch the dough but goes over the top of the bowl. Then, let it sit at room temperature for 8 to 12 hours. You are looking for a 50% increase in volume.

DOUGH 2

650g baker's flour or all-purpose flour
50g whole-grain rye flour
460g filtered warm water
17g salt

To Do:

1. Mix this dough 1 hour before dough 1 has completed its rising.
2. Allow to rest for 1 hour, and then add 17g of salt.
3. Now, mix both doughs together to make one big dough. This recipe will yield you 2 loaves or 1 big loaf.

DEVELOPMENT

1. Wet your hands slightly so the dough doesn't always stick to your hands.
2. Use the 'slap and fold' technique to develop the gluten in your dough for about 5 to 6 minutes. Then set aside to ferment for 3 to 4 hours at room temperature with 2 folds during this time.
3. Divide the dough into 750g pieces and pre-shape. Bench rest for 20 minutes. Shape the loaf again, tucking all the corners in, and then place it in your proofing basket. This is the final proofing stage. Your dough will rest here for approximately 2 hours. You can also do this for 1 hour and then place it in the fridge overnight if you would like to bake the next day.

BAKING

1. Preheat your oven to 460°F with your baking pan or Dutch oven inside it. Once everything is preheated, remove your pan from the oven, line it with parchment paper and place your dough on the paper. Make slices on the top of your dough so air can escape without bursting through the sides of your loaf. Place in the oven with your lid on the Dutch oven. If you don't have a Dutch oven, simply add a little pool of water or ice cubes under the parchment paper. The idea here is to get a crispy crust, and for that, you need moisture. Bakers often mist the bread with water using a spray bottle during the first 20 minutes of baking.
2. Bake for 20 minutes with the lid on. Remove the lid and then continue baking for another 10 to 20 minutes until your loaf is deep brown. A fully cooked loaf will have an internal temperature of 210°F.
3. Cool your bread completely before cutting it.

Other goodies you can make with sourdough starters include bagels, cookies, pancakes or waffles, muffins, and other types of bread, such as baguettes.

Welcoming a sourdough culture into your home is great for the whole family. Get your children involved if you have them. They can have the chore of feeding the sourdough starter daily or even making healthy and nutritious carbohydrates for the whole family.

SOURDOUGH BAGEL RECIPE

What you'll need:

50g active starter (lots of bubbles)
250g water
24g cane sugar
500g bread flour
11g salt
Pastry brush
1 egg for brushing

To Do:

1. Mix all your ingredients well, and make sure to work the dough well for better gluten structure. Allow the dough to sit for an hour with a wet cloth on top.
2. After one hour, work the dough again and set it aside for 8 to 10 hours or until the dough doubles in size.
3. Using a scale, divide your dough into eight parts; they should be roughly 100g each. This ensures you will have uniform bagels. Form each portion of dough, place them into a bowl covered with a damp towel and allow to rest for 10 minutes.
4. Use your thumb and index finger to punch a hole through each ball of dough and stretch it slowly while creating your bagel size. Place each bagel on a greased pan with parchment paper, and allow to proof in a warm spot for 20 minutes.
5. While your bagels are proofing, bring 4 litres of water and a tablespoon of honey to a boil. Whisk one egg in a bowl and set aside, along with a pastry brush.
6. Gently pick up each bagel and place it in the boiling water for 30 seconds on each side. Remove with a slotted ladle, and place on the baking sheet.
7. Brush each bagel with egg wash, then dip it onto your favourite bagel topper. See our Wild Everything Bagel Topper recipe shown below.
8. Bake in a 420°F oven for 15 to 20 minutes. Enjoy! These will last on your countertop for about 3 days. Store them in the fridge or freezer.

Nettle Seeds

WINTER

WILD EVERYTHING BAGEL TOPPER

What you'll need:

1 tablespoon dried nodding onions
2 tablespoons dried nettles
Dash of cayenne
Salt and pepper
1 tablespoon white sesame seeds
1 tablespoon black sesame seeds or other seeds.

To Do:

1. Mix everything together. Store in a jar or use right away.

Other Types of Foraging

Wild game is delicious when properly prepared in the kitchen and harvested from the forest. It is a lot leaner than beef, with little to no fat marbling through the meat. Instead, the fat is found on the outside edges of the meat. Some people think it can have a gamy flavour, as they are not used to it. This may be due to the animal being harvested during mating season, also known as rut. Using strong herbs like juniper and rosemary will help accompany its flavour.

This is actually the type of foraging I can say I grew up with. Hunting spring and fall bears with my father, falling asleep on the quad rides home as a young girl. It was often a cold but exciting trip out. We would venture to the northern tips of Canada for moose, or hunt grouse in our backyard. We also farmed chickens at home in my small northern town, Smithers. I was the fastest gutter when it came to butcher time … I think I'm slightly proud of that but I don't tell everyone. Gutting animals or seeing some blood never bothered me; it is important we know where our meat comes from, showing gratitude for the life taken. As many of us are learning of the inhumane slaughterhouses for beef, chickens, and other farmed animals, hunting is not only the most healthy meat you can consume but also the most humane.

I'm not going to start telling you how to hunt, you can learn that on YouTube and by getting your boots on the ground. But I will tell you a little bit about the species I'm familiar with hunting and what I think makes a great dish for the family. Foraging with You doesn't offer hunting and fishing tours. We only do wild plants and fungi for legality and tenure purposes. We do however have workshops to familiarize you with different fish species and how to go about harvesting them for food.

Mule Deer

MOOSE

Majestic and huge, moose are great for the hunter's eye and freezer. One per year can feed a family of 6. They are quite dark, with golden lower legs. The antlers can be another story though; seeing them clearly, that is. Taking down one moose for your family or splitting it between two families is an amazing harvest. It's not too tricky to learn how to gut an animal, skin it, and then butcher it in your home or shop. When skinning, be careful not to let the animal's hair fall onto the meat. A good butchering block, a boning knife, some helping hands, and a meat grinder is all you need. Wrap the meat up in a wax-coated paper wrap. You can also use saran wrap. Although I don't like the extra plastic, it does help with the freezer burn. Don't forget to label your game with the year harvested and the type of cut it is.

Nowadays, you need to put in for a draw to be able to hunt moose for a respectable amount of time in BC, Canada. The BC government is reducing the number of open season days for any hunter to go out and get their family a moose. That's why I moved on to deer …

DEER

Two islands in BC, Vancouver Island and Queen Charlotte's Island, are just crawling with small sitka deer. These can easily be shot from a small raft, either shoreside or inland. On the mainland, we have the bigger mule and white-tailed deer, but you run the risk of getting one with flesh-eating disease (a deer disease from the USA). Be sure to test deer meat by sending it to a lab before consumption, and shoot and harvest only healthy animals.

These guys are a bit harder to find in the bush and they are quite spookier and faster than moose, so they are not my preferred species. That being said, I will never turn down venison, ever. Be sure to keep the liver, it is actually quite sacred and powerful for the human body to consume, as well as the heart and the tongue. I haven't done much with tanning hides, but the task at hand is well worth making homemade leather. Keep the brains for tanning the hide – scrape it, stretch it, dry it, and rub fat into it (brains).

GROUSE

This was actually one of my first kills as a young girl before I even used a firearm. I hunted and killed one grouse with the stoning method; do not try this as it may cause injury. To gut a grouse, hunters usually step on the wings and pull the legs so that the breast comes out separate from the guts and the legs. Most hunters discard the guts and legs because they don't consider it to have enough meat but I think this is a waste, so I keep the bird whole. I also keep the feathers for crafts and jewelry. Using the whole animal is really a gift and a loyalty to the animal in the practice of foraging. Humans can sometimes be so wasteful, especially when it comes to other species and land. So I encourage you to use everything you can, like our First Nations do.

BLACK BEARS

In BC, you're allowed 2 bears a year. Bear hunting season opens up in the spring and closes in the summer. It opens up again in late fall when I prefer to get one that's just been vegging out on a massive blueberry patch. With bear meat, you do need to be careful of trichinosis, a parasite living within the meat of bears. Do not eat raw or medium-cooked bear meat. Always cook your bear meat well. Sending your bear to the butcher is a great choice. Ground bear on its own isn't the tastiest; have them make you pepperonis or breakfast sausages instead.

PRESERVING MEAT

For freezing meat, wrap it once or better yet, twice, with butcher's paper. You can also vacuum seal it. The second best preservation method is canning, which is very beneficial if you lack freezer space and free time when it comes to dinner. Cube up your meat, add the cubes to a mason jar with spices and salt, then pressure-can it. You can also invest in a freeze dryer, which is great for light hunting meals carried in a backpack. You can also smoke/dry your meat. I prefer to do this only with red meat and not bear meat unless braising it for long hours after.

WATER FORAGING A.K.A. FISHING

Rivers and lakes have lots of salmonids, perch, and crayfish (mini freshwater lobsters). Fish with a fly rod or with a gear rod for fish, and catch crayfish by hand or with a net. Lake fishing is best done in the spring when the ice has just melted, and the fishes are fresh and taste delicious. Be sure to pack salt and sugar when you go camping to make some delicious candied trout; finish it with a light smoke over your campfire. You can also just bake your fish whole, gut removed, on the side or over the fire, and remove the bones after it is done. This is an easy way to cook; the spine will pull away with all the rib bones attached when done correctly

From the ocean, nothing beats white fish meat like halibut or lingcod. In my opinion, the work is hard but the food is amazing and priceless. Investing in a bendy yet sturdy fish fillet knife is also very beneficial for any fish forager. Halibut will give you 4 fillets and the cheeks, whereas salmonids and other upright fish will give you 2 fillets each. If you choose to descale your fish, do so outside or in the field, not in your kitchen. Descaling your fish is very beneficial if you like to cook and eat the crispy skin. Fish skin is very delicious and nutritious for our bodies, full of healthy oils we cannot get anywhere else. Just like eating the liver and heart from the bigger game, we need to learn to eat all parts of our harvest.

Labrador Tea Wild Herbs found in higher elevation

Gear and Equipment

FOR THE CHEF

VITAMIX

I won't try to sell you a Vitamix, but it really is the best blender and tool to have by your side. Whether I'm blending wild hazelnuts for homemade Nutella, or grinding coffee or medicinal plant powders, a Vitamix is what I use. I also use it for wild berry smoothies and wild berry frozen desserts. Its warranty coverage is acceptable, and so are the smooth products it produces in my kitchen.

KNIVES

A good chef's knife is the best investment you'll ever make. Always keep it clean and ready to go. It is the knife you will hold in your hand the most throughout the day. Next is your boning knife – save your family some money, debone your chickens into small dinner pieces and create a beautiful soup stock with the bones. A strong and bendy fish fillet knife is my third most important knife in the kitchen. Whether you are fishing in the ocean or freshwater, a good fillet knife or two will go a long way in speeding up the processing time so you can get to eating. Make sure you have and know how to use steel, this will keep a sharp edge on your knives, making them safer to use.

ROLLING PIN

Always have one in the house. All pie crusts will require one, the same with cinnamon buns. You also need the rolling pin if you need to make mushroom powder by hand.

PASTRY BRUSH

This is like a paintbrush, or it can be made of silicone. You need it for bagel baking or any other pastry that needs to be brushed with egg wash. You need a pastry brush for our Nettle spanakopita recipe, as you layer the thin phyllo dough with clarified butter to create a crispy layered golden-brown treat. It can also be used to brush fat over your meats while roasting.

DEHYDRATOR

It doesn't matter the size, whether small or large, as long as it has warm air and good air flow.

FOR THE FORAGER

GPS

Returning home after a day of foraging is the number one priority; I have had friends sleep in the forest, and I have also gotten lost once or twice. That is why you need a reliable GPS, but don't just rely on technology. Learn to use a compass and also take note of the sun's direction and/or the mountain's direction. There are a few good cell phone apps that work out of reception; download those and track your steps. A GPS is also great for marking your 'spots,' as we like to call them. Fungi will appear year after year in the same spot, so we often mark their locations on a GPS so there's less footwork the following year. And lastly, tell someone where you're going or bring a friend. Two minds thinking about the way out are better than one.

BASKETS AND BUCKETS

We use baskets and buckets with holes drilled on the side when foraging for mushrooms, specifically. Mushrooms need to breathe oxygen. They also hold a lot of heat or energy after being harvested. The heat needs to escape, otherwise, it will turn your mushrooms bad. That's why we drill holes in the sides of our buckets or use a perforated basket. Harvesting mushrooms in a basket also allows the spores to drop as you walk the forest, enhancing mushroom production. In a pinch, you can use a plastic bag but don't make it a practice, as the mushrooms will get soggy.

Weaved baskets work well for nettles, lettuces, Japanese knotweed, flowers, cleavers, mushrooms, and some berry clusters. Most wild berries are very fragile, so be sure to pick them directly into a small container or ziplock bag. We now offer foraging aprons at Foraging with You, designed and made locally by us; this is a fast and easy way to pick your herbs with both hands vs. holding a bag in one hand and having to move it each time.

FORAGING KNIFE

This knife should be small, preferably foldable or stored in a sheath on your belt. The last thing you want to be carrying around is an open blade in the forest while you try to hike over and under fallen debris. I have recently found the sheath option to be the best because I return the knife back to the sheath after each use, versus a folding knife that can, sometimes, be placed on the ground and left behind.

FOOTWEAR

Ankle support is important, especially when foraging for fall mushrooms in a mossy old-growth forest. Not just the ankle support but also ankle covering, as you can quickly fall through rotten logs or branches. Gainers not only keep debris out of your socks and ankles, but also cover the shoe laces, which can be a tripping hazard. Gumboots are also a wise choice to use. They might not be the best for hiking, but they are a must when you're picking fiddleheads in the swamps or crossing creeks to get to your Japanese knotweed.

SUMMER CLOTHING

I don't care what you look like foraging, but you should have long pants and a long-sleeved shirt on so you don't get stung by nettles or scraped with branches as you chaotically make your way through the dense forest in search of gold (yes, I consider most fungi and forage items like gold). Also, consider having a baseball-style hat on your head. This doesn't just keep the bugs out of your hair, but it protects your eyes from sticks jabbing into them.

WET SEASON CLOTHING

It's well worth the investment in a good rain jacket and rain pants. Foraging can be an all-day experience in and out of the vehicle, so you need to stay dry and warm. A rain cap or canvas-style cowboy hat is also helpful in a sudden torrential downpour.

VEHICLE

You don't need to have a 4 x 4 vehicle, but it sure is handy. When foraging, dirt roads can get pretty potholey, and if it's raining, there can be a lot of mud. Foraging in a car can also be necessary, as there is always lots of driving around to be done as you look for new spots. Often I have to drive two hours out of town for my morels or asparagus harvest.

A Different Perspective

A DIFFERENT PERSPECTIVE

FROM THE MUSHROOM

Did you know I'm so much more than what you see here? There is much more to me than meets the eye. What you are holding in your hand is actually only my fruiting body. The rest of me—my mycelium, or roots, some might say—is actually beneath your feet. Well, not directly beneath your feet, but under the moss and forest debris. My mycelium is connected to other mycelium networks, tree networks, plant networks, and all the other microorganisms that you call the forest. We all talk to each other, you see. I'm never lonely.

Please harvest me gently. Use your hands to gently move the earth away if needed, then cut my stem with a knife. This ensures that my mycelium root structure will not be disrupted. After you harvest me, tap my little head so that my extra spores will fall out onto the ground, where they belong. Dust off any debris, then place me in a bag or basket that has holes so I can breathe. That's right—mushrooms like to breathe oxygen, just like humans; we're more alike than you know. Before you leave the forest (or some people do it before they pick me), leave a little offering of herbs or tobacco on the ground as a symbol of gratitude to the mushrooms and the forest.

I can be picky when it comes to weather. I like the temperature to be hot but not too hot. I also must have moisture—every mushroom needs a drink of water, don't they? If those August or September rains don't come, or if it gets cold too early, I will not come out to play. Some would say that's not being a fun-gi . . .

FROM THE FOREST

I am awake. I am alive. Hello to you, too. I will always welcome you with open branches, although I cannot guarantee protection. Many humans and creatures enjoy my healing vibrational energy. Did you know if you hug a tree, it can help you clear your mind, calm your heart, and make you feel like a million bucks? Be sure to ask for permission first, my dear friend, as the trees are sentient beings. In fact, all plants, berries, and mushrooms are.

If you dare to take those things you call shoes off your feet, you will feel the vibrational frequency of the Earth. This is called grounding in your language. It reduces inflammation, anxiety, and stress, and it boosts your immune system. That is why you're here, isn't it? To heal your body with food from the forest? So why not take off your shoes and get some real healing? Enjoy your time here, taking what you need for yourself and others to use as medicine or food. Be sure to use your manners, and give a gift back as you take, and take. The plants enjoy gifts of herbs, crystals, tobacco, or even just a hair from your head, as traditionally done by many ancients.

If you would be so kind, consider this message from the great elders of all Tree Beings: "We appreciate the replanting humans do after logging, but this planet cannot withstand much more destruction of old-growth forests. These forests are home to our largest and oldest trees as well as very sophisticated mycelium networks. Old-growth forests also take in copious amounts of CO_2 from the atmosphere, a service every creature on Earth needs. Thank you in advance for doing all you can to spread awareness of this issue."

A DIFFERENT PERSPECTIVE

FROM THE BERRIES

First I flower, oh so pretty. Then I die and find my true juicy self: a wild berry! While I am still a flower, you can pick my petals and use them fresh or dried as an elegant decoration for cakes and cupcakes. Be warned, though, if you take the whole flower bud, there will be no berry in that spot. Remember, we are an important nutrient for our fellow birds, squirrels, bears, and other creatures. So take only what you need, and leave the rest to reseed and feed nature.

There are many different shapes of berries, just like there are many different shapes of humans. The wild salmonberry has one seed per drupelet, like your common red raspberry. Speaking of raspberries, there are wild raspberries called blackcaps. They are quite a bit darker than your conventional red ones, but they are delicious nevertheless. Other berries are round with a small bundle of seeds in the middle. We are jampacked with antioxidants, vitamins, and other nutrients. Enjoy us on your trail hikes, or join us when we are in abundance and pick many of us to bring home. We can be found at high and low elevations all over the world. Many of the edible berries are red, blue, or purple—but stay away from the white snowberry, please; those are not for you to eat. Always know for sure, for sure, for sure what you are picking and eating.

A DIFFERENT PERSPECTIVE

FROM THE HERBS

Hello, I'm down here! We are the smallest of all the forest plants, unless it is summer—then some of us wild herbs grow really tall. Some of us, such as self-heal, have flowers, and others, such as the stinging nettle, just produce seeds. We can be enjoyed as a culinary delight, the way your ancestors used to do, adding high levels of nutrients to your food. Or you can use us for medicinal purposes, also done by your ancestors. Whatever the case, be sure to give us kind words of thanks or a gift of your choice so we can be at peace when picked and happy to come home to be used as medicine.

The forest often will give you what you need, not want. Try infusing us and making yourself a medicinal healing salve or tincture. Make your potions with dry or fresh herbs; we are all here to help mankind on its journey. When you cut trails or do yard maintenance, please remember that we are sentient beings as well. We are resilient, but our feelings still get hurt. Don't spray us with lawn chemicals; this will only harm the planet and yourself. Dandelions are a very beneficial herb that could improve your health, yet many of you spray glyphosate on them, harming not only the plant but also the bees and other pollinators that depend on them. If you kill all the pollinators, wild and domesticated plants will not be able to pollinate and grow to serve your highest needs. So be warned, take care of us and do not spray us if the effects of your actions are unknown.

Final Note from The Author

My first ever mushroom harvest was in Tofino, BC, for golden chanterelle mushrooms. This was a pure delight after always seeing these beauties in the kitchen where I worked locally. I even got lost my first time foraging by depending on someone else to bring us out of the bush. After that, I was unstoppable! I worked at a heli-ski lodge through the winter, and would self-study and forage during the other months. One spring, I hit the road to live in the forests of Tumbler Ridge, BC, with other mushroom pickers, hunting for the amazing morel mushroom. I then continued mushroom picking into the Yukon, where the mushrooms got even bigger!

I do hope you enjoyed this book of recipes and the tricks I have learned in the cheffing and foraging industries. Foraging has given me much self-empowerment with my home food culture, and I hope it can do the same for you. I love not having to go to the grocery store in the spring when I can fill my kitchen with wild foods I gathered on casual walks. I love the seasonal adventure of going mushroom picking in the fall, or asparagus picking and lake fishing in spring. Eating with the seasons is such a pure joy. I anticipate the arrival of spring with excitement, knowing I will soon be making a sweet asparagus soup. Fresh morels? Who can beat that? I am eating the best food on Earth. That is what I hope to bring people into alignment with: eating the best food on earth for little to no cost while connecting them back to nature. Hunting and gathering are in your blood and DNA; I hope this book will inspire you to return to that heritage.

Foraging is a process. Every season, you will learn more and more about how to use your goodies in different ways and become more comfortable with different fungi, and veggies, and their uses. Soon, you will have a pantry infused with wild medicinal goods. It will take a few years, a few books, and, yes, a lot of footwork as you explore dead ends and find your spots. But after about 5 years, you will be set!

About the Author

Raeanna Layfield, a Canadian Red Seal chef, traded the hectic kitchen life for the tranquillity of the forest. Growing up with a passion for hunting and fishing, she delved into gourmet cooking in her twenties. Fascinated by wild mushrooms and veggies in restaurant kitchens, she embarked on foraging adventures.

In 2020, she founded "Foraging with You," a chef-inspired wild food company based in BC, Canada, teaching clients to safely gather and cook edible, medicinal wild plants and fungi. Offering tours and workshops, Raeanna emphasizes the health and cultural benefits of foraging, aligning with nature's seasons.

She's written this book to deepen people's connection with nature and self-sustenance.

If you are ever unsure, or want to deepen your knowledge with an in-person tour, we are here for you, offering foraging tours during all the seasons. We also offer cooking classes and live chef dinners in your home. Our tours include a wild seasonal snack, and a wild hot or iced tea depending on the season. We have gourmet tours that bring you out of town for asparagus or wild onions and these tours include a full wild food lunch! I continue to create more fun workshops connecting people back to nature, like our Plant Wave Workshop, Goddess Circles timed with the cycles of the moon and our Foraging and Feast Experience, where you get to enjoy your forage cooked over a live fire by me, your chef. We have also teamed up with a truffle farm and are offering Truffle Forays in BC Canada.

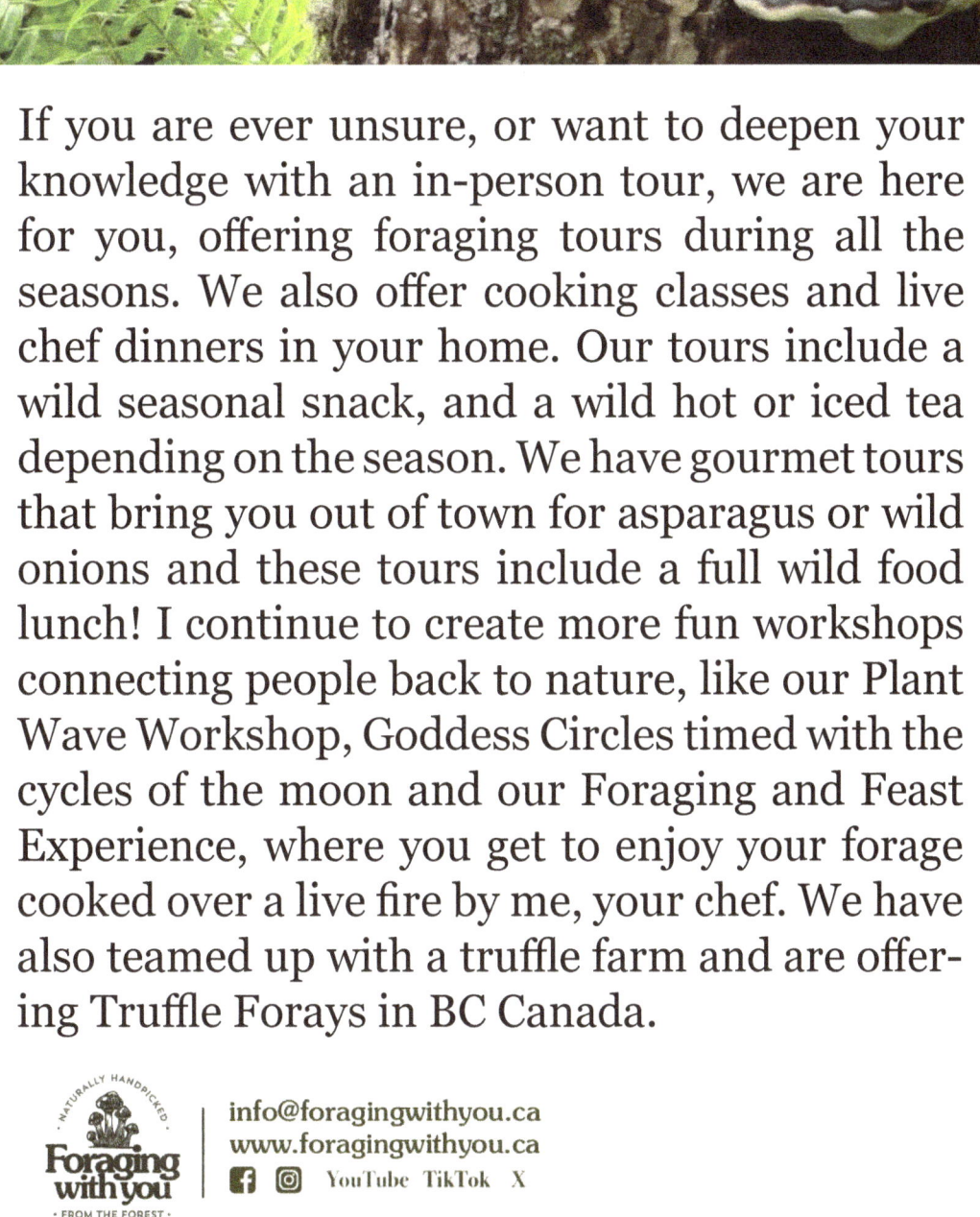

info@foragingwithyou.ca
www.foragingwithyou.ca
YouTube TikTok X

www.ingramcontent.com/pod-product-compliance
Lightning Source LLC
Chambersburg PA
CBHW042357070526
44585CB00029B/2971